GHOSTLY ENCOUNTERS

TERRIFYING TALES OF PARANORMAL ENCOUNTERS

Publications International, Ltd.

Contributing Writers: Jeff Bahr, Fiona Broome, Tom DeMichael, Linda Godfrey, J. K. Kelley, Patricia Martinelli, Suzanne Reisman, Michael Riedlinger, Russ Roberts, Lawrence Robinson, Adam Selzer, Sue Sveum, Donald Vaughan, James Willis

Factual Verification: Hollie Deese, Kathryn L. Holcomb, Carl Miller, Christy Nadalin

Cover Illustration: Shutterstock

Interior Illustrations: Art Explosion, iStockphoto, Jupiterimages

ISBN-13: 978-1-4508-6354-4
ISBN-10: 1-4508-6354-X

Manufactured in China.

8 7 6 5 4 3 2 1

CONTENTS

Are You a Believer?

Do you believe in ghosts? Most people have never seen a ghost, and for many seeing is believing. But that doesn't mean that ghosts don't exist. What if there is more to this world than meets the eye? Indeed, there is growing evidence that a spiritual realm exists beyond our physical world.

Whether you're a believer or a skeptic, *Ghostly Encounters* will get your heart pounding with a host of ghost stories and terrifying tales of the paranormal. These are true tales (or so we're told) of the weird and wicked, the spectral and spirited, the creepy and cryptic. Some are intriguing, some are funny, and some will have you scratching your head in disbelief. But don't say we didn't warn you. The stories in this book may give you chills or thrills. And after reading a tale or two, you may even feel the urge to sleep with the hall light on, look under your bed, or double-check that the closet door is closed before you go to sleep—you know, *just in case.*

Ghostly Encounters will tempt you and tease you with freaky and frightening facts as well as scary stories of visits from the "Other Side."

Still skeptical? Here's a taste of what we have in store for you:

• A ghost named Annette haunts a restaurant in New York. Annette can be playful, but she can also be mischievous— she once threw a drink in a diner's face!

- A spectral boy is just one of the spirits who haunts Waverly Hills Sanatorium in Louisville, Kentucky. He likes to play with visitors by rolling a ball across the floor or moving it from room to room.

- The Lemp Mansion in St. Louis has seen more than its share of tragedy over the years, so it's no surprise that many mournful spirits still linger there. Visitors have seen glasses fly through the air, chairs move on their own, and candles light themselves. A ghost dog even haunts the place!

- In Chicago, the restless spirits at a funeral-home-turned-tattoo-parlor taunted a former owner and may have frightened him into an early grave.

- In the basement of Bobby Mackey's nightclub in Wilder, Kentucky, there's a well that's rumored to be a portal to the Other Side. The headless ghost of Pearl Bryan also haunts the place, as do her angry killers, who may be responsible for attacks on some patrons.

See what we mean? That's some scary stuff! Sure, nobody really knows what happens after death, but once you've read the stories in *Ghostly Encounters,* it's hard to deny that there are some strange and unexplainable things going on out there. So sit back, relax, and get ready for a wild and scary ride!

You Might Have a Ghost if...

In order to determine if a place is haunted, you must first rule out any logical explanations for weird things that are happening there. Strange noises might just be signs of bad plumbing or rodents in the house. But if there's no reasonable explanation for what's going on, you might have a ghost. Here are a few telltale signs of a haunting.

You Hear Unexplained Noises

If you hear weird noises in the house—such as scratching or banging sounds, knocks, distant music, muffled voices, or disembodied footsteps—and there's no logical reason for them, you may be sharing your home with a ghost.

Items Disappear and Reappear Later in a Different Place

In this phenomenon, an object comes up missing only to be found later in an entirely different location. Or an item disappears from its regular location, then shows up there some time later. It's as if the ghost is playing a game of keep away just for the thrill of driving you crazy.

Objects Operate Without Human Assistance

Ghosts like to play games and make their presence known. They might do this by opening and closing doors and turning lights, TVs, radios, electrical appliances, or even battery-operated toys on and off. A toilet flushing on its own can be a sign that you have a plumbing problem, but it's also one of the most common tricks in the ghost handbook.

If you've ruled out all scientific reasons for the strange stuff, you might have an otherworldly visitor.

You Smell Unexplained Odors

A ghost might make its presence known by giving off a whiff of a scent that it was known for in life. This could be the smell of a favorite perfume or cologne, a favorite food, cigar smoke, or even body odor. Like most ghosts, the scent will vanish as quickly as it arrived.

You Experience Cold Spots or Weird Temperature Changes

Paranormal researchers believe that ghosts need energy to make their presence known to the living. A cold spot is thought to be an area where a ghost has drained away the heat energy. A cold spot is often about ten degrees cooler than the surrounding area and is about the size of a human. If you're hit with a sudden chill that quickly passes through you, you may have just crossed paths with a ghost. Spirits can also show themselves by giving off heat, just as a human would, but such cases are very rare.

Fraidycats and Paranoid Pooches

Animals have more finely tuned senses than humans. And many paranormal researchers believe that animals— especially dogs—can see spirits even when humans cannot. So if your faithful pooch barks or growls (or your cat hisses) at thin air, he might see something that you can't. If your pet suddenly refuses to enter a certain room or seems to be following something with his eyes, he might be trying to tell you that there's a g-g-g-ghost in the room!

"I Always Feel Like Somebody's Watching Me"

When in the presence of a ghost, many people can sense that something unseen is nearby. It's also common to feel like you're being watched. Some people even experience the sensation that someone has touched their hair, tapped them on the shoulder, nudged them, or whispered in their ear. But if an invisible presence scratches you, slaps you, or causes you physical harm, that's a clear sign that you're dealing with an unfriendly spirit or a demon. Don't try to deal with it on your own. Seek professional help immediately.

You See Strange Shadows or Actual Apparitions

If you see misty shapes or fleeting shadows that aren't attached to anyone or anything in particular, you've probably got a ghost. It is believed that such forms are spirits that don't have the energy to manifest into full-blown apparitions. Many ghosts have detailed facial features and distinct clothing, and some look so real that you only know you've seen a ghost when it disappears before your very eyes!

A MURDERED WIFE'S REVENGE

Louisa Luetgert tormented her killer from the Other Side. Did she also coax him into an early grave?

In the late 1800s, Adolph Luetgert owned a sausage-making company in Chicago. Adolph's business did quite well in the beginning, but then it fell on hard times. As a result, Adolph's marriage to his wife, Louisa, began to suffer, and their arguments grew increasingly intense. Then, on May 1, 1897, Louisa simply disappeared. Adolph told detectives that she had left him, but Louisa's brother didn't buy it. He pressed the police to continue their investigation.

THE EVIDENCE MOUNTS

When police questioned the Luetgerts' neighbors and relatives, they heard about violent arguments and abuse. Finally, a witness came forward to say that she had seen Adolph leading Louisa down the alley behind the sausage factory on the night she disappeared.

The police also questioned Adolph's employees. A security guard told them that on May 2 at around 3 A.M., he saw Adolph working in the basement. Later that same morning, the guard saw a sticky, gluelike substance near the vat. He noticed that it seemed to contain bits of bone, but he thought nothing of it. After all, Adolph used all sorts of waste meats to make his sausage, so the guard assumed that's what it was.

Detectives eventually found some receipts that proved Adolph had purchased large amounts of arsenic and potash (a dissolving agent) the day before Louisa disappeared. They also heard rumors that the financially strapped sausage king had been secretly dating a wealthy widow, and he planned to marry her after Louisa was out of the picture.

Putting two and two together, the detectives concluded that Adolph had killed his wife, dissolved her body in potash, and then burned what was left of her remains in the factory's furnace. A few weeks into the investigation, the police searched the factory's basement, where they found a vat that was two-thirds full of a brownish liquid. When the officers drained the greasy slime from the vat, they uncovered several bone fragments and two gold rings—one was engraved with the initials "L. L."

HAUNTED IN THE BIG HOUSE

After a very public trial, Adolph Luetgert was found guilty of murdering Louisa and was sentenced to life in prison. While behind bars, he repeatedly told prison guards that the ghost of his dead wife was haunting him, exacting her revenge for a crime that he still claimed he did not commit. Adolph died in prison in 1899.

LINGERING LOUISA

Meanwhile, several witnesses reported that Louisa's ghost had taken up residence in the Luetgerts' former home and was sometimes seen leaning against the fireplace mantel. The house was later rented out, but tenants didn't stay long. They complained that the ghost of Louisa Luetgert—who was apparently still angry about her untimely death—refused to leave them in peace.

Eventually, the factory was sold and the home was moved to a different location in the neighborhood. In the late 1990s—around the 100th anniversary of Louisa's death—the former sausage factory was converted into condominiums. Fashionable brick homes and trendy coffee shops popped up nearby, replacing the aging relics from the Luetgerts' era.

But one thing has not changed: Legend has it that each year on May 1, a ghostly Louisa Luetgert can be seen walking down the street near the old sausage factory. Perhaps she's reliving the final moments of her life.

"The murdered do haunt their murderers, I believe. I know that ghosts have wandered on earth. Be with me always—take any form—drive me mad!"

—Emily Brontë, *Wuthering Heights*

THE SMURL INCIDENT

*In the 1970s, the "Amityville Horror" story ignited a
firestorm of controversy that's still discussed
today. The Smurl haunting may not be as
well known, but it is just as debatable.*

SPIRIT RUMBLINGS

In 1973, Jack and Janet Smurl and their daughters Dawn and
Heather moved into a duplex in West Pittston, Pennsylvania.
Jack's parents occupied one side of the duplex and Jack and
Janet took the other. Nothing unusual occurred during the
first 18 months that they lived there, but then odd things
started to happen. Claw marks were found on the bathtub,
the sink, and the woodwork. An unexplained stain appeared
on the carpet. A television burst into flames. And Dawn saw
people floating in her bedroom.

In 1977, Jack and Janet welcomed twin daughters Shannon
and Carin to the family. By then, the home had become
Spook Central. Unplugged radios played, drawers opened
and closed with no assistance, toilets flushed on their own,
empty porch chairs rocked back and forth, and horrible
smells circulated throughout the house.

By 1985, events at the Smurl home had taken a dangerous
turn. The house was always cold, and Jack's parents often
heard angry voices coming from their son's side of the
duplex, even though Jack and Janet were not arguing.

In February of that year, Janet was alone in the kitchen when the room became frigid. Then suddenly, a faceless, black, human-shaped form appeared. It floated through the wall and Jack's mother saw it too.

At this point, the situation became even more bizarre. On the night that Heather was confirmed into the Catholic faith, Shannon was nearly killed when a large light fixture fell from the ceiling and landed on her. On another night, Janet was violently pulled off the bed. Jack was lying right next to her, but he was unable to help her as a foul odor nearly suffocated him. Sometimes, heavy footsteps were heard in the attic, and knocking and scratching sounds came from the walls. Not even the family dog escaped: It was repeatedly picked up and thrown around.

"WHO YOU GONNA CALL?"

Unwilling to be terrorized out of their home, the Smurls contacted psychic researchers and demonologists Ed and Lorraine Warren in January 1986. The Warrens confirmed that four evil spirits, including a powerful demon, were haunting the home. The Warrens believed that the emotions generated as the older Smurl daughters entered puberty had somehow awakened a dormant demon.

The Warrens tried prayer and playing religious music, but that only angered the demon even more. It wrote "Get out of this house" on a mirror, violently shook drawers, filled the

TV set with an eerie white light, and slapped and bit Jack and Janet.

One day, Janet decided to try communicating with the demon on her own. She told it to knock once if it was there to harm them. It knocked once. Later, Carin fell seriously ill with a high fever. And pig noises—which supposedly signal the presence of a demon—came from the walls.

The Smurls could not escape even by leaving their home. The creature followed them on camping trips and even bothered Jack at his job. The family asked the Catholic Church for help but to no avail. However, a priest named Robert F. McKenna did try to help the Smurls by performing an exorcism in the spring of 1986, but even that didn't help.

Going Public

Finally, in August 1986, the Smurls told their story to the media. The incidents continued, but the publicity got the attention of Paul Kurtz, chairman of the Committee for the Scientific Investigation of Claims of the Paranormal (CSICOP). He offered to investigate, but the Smurls turned him down, stating that they wanted to stay with the Warrens and the Church. They were also concerned that CSICOP had already decided that their story was a hoax.

The Smurls did contact a medium who came to the same conclusion as the Warrens—that there were four spirits in the home. One she couldn't identify, but she said that the others were an old woman named Abigail, a murderer named Patrick, and a very strong demon.

Another exorcism was performed in the summer of 1986, and that seemed to do the trick because the incidents stopped...or so it seemed. Just before Christmas of that year, the black form appeared again, along with the banging noises, the foul odors, and other phenomena.

SURRENDER

The Smurls finally moved out of the home in 1988. The next owner said that she never experienced any supernatural events while she lived there.

That same year, *The Haunted*, a book based on the Smurl family's experiences, was released. And in 1991, a TV movie with the same title aired.

But the controversy surrounding the alleged haunting was just beginning. In an article written for *The Skeptical Inquirer*, CSICOP's official magazine, Paul Kurtz cited money from the book deal as a reason to doubt the Smurls's story. He also said that for years, residents in the area had complained about terrible odors coming from a sewer pipe. He cited other natural explanations for some incidents and raised questions about others. He further claimed that the Warrens gave him a number of conflicting reasons for why he couldn't see the video and audio evidence that they said they'd collected.

And that's where matters stand today—with those who believe in the Smurl family's account on one side and the doubters on the other. Just like the Amityville incident, the Smurl haunting is likely to be debated for a long time to come.

THE GLOWING STUDENT

A tragic kitchen accident gave life to a ghost that continues to haunt…and she's not alone.

In 1908, Condie Cunningham was a fun-loving student at the Alabama Girls Industrial School (now known as the University of Montevallo). She was cooking with friends in her dormitory's kitchen when flammable cleaning solvent accidentally spilled onto the stove. Condie's clothing caught on fire, burning her severely. She died in a hospital two days later.

More than a century later, Condie's tortured spirit still haunts Main Hall, where the terrible accident took place. Witnesses report hearing her desperate cries for help, and a few people have even seen her ghost running through the building, glowing brightly as if on fire.

That's the assumption, anyway. In almost every account, witnesses said that they saw a flash of red—like fire—out of the corner of their eye, but when they turned around to get a better look, there was nothing there.

College Spirit(s)

Several other spirits are said to haunt the hallowed halls of the University of Montevallo. In Reynolds Hall, one female student was reportedly kicked by an unseen force. Ghosts also haunt both of the school's theaters, where doors swing open by themselves, windows open and close on their own, and odd noises come from the attic above one of the stages.

School historians believe one of the theater-bound specters may be Henry Clay Reynolds, the college's first president. Another theater-loving ghost is thought to be Walter Trumbauer, a former drama instructor who—according to legend—often appears during College Night, an annual competition of student-performed musical theater. Supposedly, Trumbauer makes his presence known by causing a board above the stage to sway over the performer who will win the contest. Once a drama teacher, always a drama teacher—even in the afterlife.

The Haunted Toy Store

A California Toys"R"Us is home to a playful spirit.

With a cheerful name like Sunnyvale, this midsize town in California's Silicon Valley may seem like an odd place for a haunting. But stranger still is the location being haunted:

a popular Toys"R"Us store. Employees say that something unseen routinely wreaks havoc there after they have left for the night.

The actions of the mischievous spirit seem almost like things that a spoiled child would do. Books are tossed on the floor and roller skates are scattered all about, even though everything was put away when employees locked up the night before.

Sometimes the ghost gets more personal. More than one employee has reportedly been tapped on the shoulder only to find no one there, and several female employees have felt unseen hands touch their hair. And there was the time that a group of employees rolled down a metal door in the store and then heard someone yelling and pounding from the other side. When they rolled the door back up, no one was there.

Psychic Encounter

In 1978, famous psychic Sylvia Brown visited the store hoping to make contact with the silly spook and figure out who it was in life. Sylvia said she saw a tall, thin man wearing a coat. He said his name was Johnny Johnson. During their chat, Johnny told Sylvia that she should move or her feet would get wet. This confused her until further research revealed that there had once been a well where she was standing.

The store hasn't tried to scare away the prankster phantom. In fact, most of the employees are fond—even protective— of Johnny, and very few feel scared or threatened by him. And whether he's just a little clumsy or he simply wants to have fun, it seems that he's in the right place. After all, what better place is there to have some fun than a toy store?

DEAD MEN TELL TALES

In recent years, Americans have gone gaga over pirates. Perhaps the most famous buccaneer of all was Edward Teach, better known as Blackbeard. His career was built on fear and intimidation, and apparently he hasn't changed—not even in death.

THE DEVIL OF THE DEEP BLUE SEA

Blackbeard's reign of terror on the high seas lasted for more than two years. During that time, he commanded a fleet of captured vessels and attacked any ship he pleased. He thieved and murdered up and down the East Coast until he turned himself in and was pardoned in July 1718.

After receiving his pardon, it didn't take long for Blackbeard to return to a life of piracy. In November 1718, Virginia Governor Alexander Spotswood ordered Lieutenant Robert Maynard to capture Blackbeard. On November 22, Maynard and his men caught up with the famed pirate and his crew just off Ocracoke Island in present-day North Carolina. Blackbeard and Maynard exchanged gunfire, and then the men drew their swords. Blackbeard managed to break Maynard's blade, but before he could kill the officer, a member of Maynard's party slit Blackbeard's throat. It took a total of 5 gunshot wounds and 20 sword strokes to bring down the notorious pirate. And just to ensure that he was dead, his head was cut off and hung from Maynard's ship.

Home Is Where the Head Is

Since that fateful day, Blackbeard's bloody specter has been seen on Ocracoke Island carrying a lantern, apparently searching for his missing head. The island is known locally as "Teach's Hole," and visitors and residents alike have reported seeing his phantom swimming along the shore at night. Some have even watched him rise up from his watery grave and continue his search along the shore. Fishermen have dubbed any strange lights seen on North Carolina's Outer Banks "Teach's Lights." The few souls brave enough to follow the unearthly glow of Blackbeard's lantern ashore never find footprints or other signs of life when they investigate. But try as he might to find his missing head, some legends suggest that Blackbeard is looking for his noggin in the wrong place.

Death to Spotswood!

In the 1930s, North Carolina judge Charles Whedbee claimed to have seen Blackbeard's skull. According to him, when he was in law school, he was invited to join a secret society. His induction into the group involved a large silver cup and the chanting of the mysterious phrase "Death to Spotswood." Whedbee was told that a silversmith had made the cup from Blackbeard's skull after stealing it from atop a pole more than two centuries before. The macabre goblet seems to have been lost, but it isn't the only treasure that Blackbeard is said to have left behind.

BLACKBEARD'S LADY

Another legend suggests that during his reign of terror, Blackbeard left two treasures on Lunging Island, which is located off the coast of New Hampshire. One was a large amount of silver; the other was his wife, Mary Ormond. Over the years, several people have tried to find the missing treasure, but always to no avail. However, many people have encountered the wispy figure of a woman wandering along the beach at night. Legend has it that she was Blackbeard's wife and that she was left behind to guard his loot.

When Blackbeard returned to North Carolina in 1718, he was offered a pardon and was also granted Mary Ormond's hand in marriage. The pirate tried to settle down with Mary, but clearly, domestic life was not for him. The excitement of looting on the high seas got the best of him, and it was there that he met his doom shortly thereafter.

Blackbeard never returned to Lunging Island—at least not while he was alive. Although the ghostly woman is said to whisper, "He will return," she apparently doesn't recognize the headless specter that also reportedly wanders the island.

Ghostly Encounters of the Average Joe

There's something fascinating about a ghost story. And sometimes the scariest tales are the personal encounters that regular people—people just like you—have with the paranormal. The following accounts were shared on the television show My Ghost Story. *They'll leave you wondering what* you'd *do if you encountered a ghost.*

Footprints on the Bed

Unexplained noises and cabinet doors opening on their own were the first clues that Marci Smith's home in Maryland might be haunted. And it only got worse from there. She felt something move across her feet at night, but there were no signs of rodents, so she set up a video camera to record her bedroom while she was sleeping. What she captured convinced her that something otherworldly was sharing her house. A misty figure that looked like a phantom cat was seen jumping onto the bed. Later in the video, the blankets moved as if an unseen presence was walking across the bed.

Marci called in paranormal investigators, who set up audio and video recorders in the house. Several voices were captured, ranging from children to elderly people. Marci said that the house seems perfectly normal during the daytime. But at night? Well, let's just say that she's never really alone.

One Cool Spirit

If anyone would be safe from a ghostly encounter, it would surely be someone in the security business, right? Wrong. One night, Ron Colbert (a policeman of nearly 24 years) and a coworker were monitoring security cameras in an office building when Ron saw a ghostly orb move across the deserted lobby of a bank. They cleaned the camera, adjusted the blinds, moved a chair, and finally replaced the camera in an effort to debunk the phenomenon. But the orb kept coming back, and employees became spooked. The lobby was also the coldest room in the building, with temperatures never rising above 60°F. After space heaters were brought in to warm up the room, the orb was never seen again.

The Spirited Giraffe

When Nicholas Honkoski's father acquired a two-foot-tall porcelain giraffe statue from Africa, life started to get a little weird in the family's house in San Gabriel, California. Nick and his cousin Cody heard strange noises, so they decided to set up a video camera to record while they were sleeping. When they watched the footage, they saw the giraffe moving across the floor by itself! The camera even captured a partial apparition: a ghostly arm that reached out to grab Cody. The pair also picked up EVPs (electronic voice phenomena), and Cody saw the reflection of Nick's deceased grandfather in a mirror. One morning, the giraffe figurine was found shattered. After that, everything returned to normal. The cousins never did figure out the connection between the giraffe and the spirit world, but they were relieved when the haunting stopped.

AN ORDINARY GUY MEETS A LONG-DEAD ACTRESS

When David Oman built a house next to the site where five people were brutally murdered in 1969, he was "welcomed" by a few uninvited guests. During his first night in his new home, David awoke to see the full-bodied apparition of a man. He got up to investigate, and when he asked who was there, he was shocked to hear, "It's Sharon." That would be Sharon Tate, the actress who was eight-and-a-half months pregnant when she was brutally murdered by Charles Manson's followers. Items that disappear and reappear in other places, objects that crash to the ground on their own, and a photo showing an orb within an orb (indicating a pregnant spirit) are just some of the things David has encountered there. He's learned to live with his invisible roommates, but his friends prefer to hang out elsewhere.

Ghosts on the Silver Screen

*Ghosts and other creepy creatures have been showing
up in movies since the late 1890s. Here are some
of the most popular spooky stories on film.*

The Shining (1980)

Based on a novel by Stephen King, *The Shining* initially
seems to be pure fiction. However, King based the story on
his stay at the Stanley Hotel in Estes Park, Colorado. King
has said that he hates the film, but it really packs a punch.
Jack Nicholson portrays a caretaker who is influenced by the
evil forces in the hotel. You may have been afraid of your dad
at some point, but has he ever chased you with an ax?

Poltergeist (1982)

Horror director Tobe Hooper teamed up with Steven
Spielberg to create *Poltergeist*—one of the most successful
haunted house movies ever. The film is based on a story
by Spielberg and is remembered for its extra-nimble clown
doll and the famous line, "They're *heeeere!*" The film and
its sequel are famously rumored to have been cursed. The
"*Poltergeist* Curse" allegedly took the lives of four cast members within six years of the original film's release, including
child star Heather O'Rourke, who died tragically at age 12,
and Dominique Dunne, who was murdered by her boyfriend
at age 22.

THE BLAIR WITCH PROJECT (1999)

This hugely successful film became a sensation largely because of a marketing campaign that tried to convince viewers that the events depicted in the film had actually happened. But still, the slow stalking of Heather, Mike, and Josh by a never-seen presence offers bona fide chills, to say nothing of the nausea brought on by the jittery camera work. Although the truth was eventually revealed, many people believed that the movie was composed of actual footage shot by three hikers who went missing in the woods in Maryland.

THE HAUNTING IN CONNECTICUT (2009)

The Haunting in Connecticut is based on the experiences of the Snedeker family of Southington, Connecticut. When Carmen Snedeker moved her family into a former funeral home, she had no idea that they would deal with moving dishes or buckets in which water turned blood red. Contrary to the film, the Snedekers didn't discover bodies or burn the house down. Eventually, like many haunting victims, they simply moved out of the house. Despite the exaggerated Hollywood ending, it seems that everything else shown in the film actually happened to the Snedekers.

PARANORMAL ACTIVITY (2009)

Made on a budget estimated to be only $15,000, Oren Peli's *Paranormal Activity* looks authentic, but it's simply a believable work of film fiction. Peli channeled his own fear of ghosts to create a frightening flick that feels like a true haunting. The film arouses the fear felt by anyone living in a home that truly is haunted.

PENANCE FOR YOUR SINS

It began as a unique place to help reform prisoners. It ended up being a torture chamber where men often met agonizing deaths. Sadly, many of those tormented souls have been unable to leave the Eastern State Penitentiary—even in death.

THE ROAD TO PENANCE

The Eastern State Penitentiary was truly a unique experiment in the history of law enforcement. It was different from other prisons because it was meant to stress reform rather than punishment. It was thought that by giving a prisoner plenty of time to reflect on his wrongdoing, he would eventually reform himself by turning to God to make penance—hence the word *penitentiary.*

In October 1829, when the Eastern State Penitentiary officially opened in Philadelphia, it was one of the largest public buildings of its kind in the United States. Its unique features blew prisoners and employees away. For starters, the entire complex looked like a giant wagon wheel, with seven wings of cells emerging from the center like spokes.

ISOLATION AND MADNESS

Unlike most prisons of the time, each cell was designed to house only one inmate. The idea was that prisoners needed time to reflect on what they had done wrong, and giving them cell mates would only distract them from doing that.

Additionally, inmates were only allowed to interact with the warden, who visited every prisoner once a day, and the guards, who served meals and brought inmates to and from their cells. Prisoners were permitted to go outside for exercise, but they could only do so alone. When an inmate was removed from his cell for any reason, he had to wear a hood over his head. Prisoners were to remain silent at all times unless asked a direct question by prison personnel. Breaking this rule led to harsh and ruthless punishment.

TORTUROUS BEHAVIOR

Although the facility's intent may have been to get inmates to understand that they needed to follow the rules in order to be reformed, that quickly broke down into brutality by the guards. Minor offenses, including making even the slightest noise, were cause for horrific punishments. Restraint devices such as straitjackets and the "mad chair" were often used. (The mad chair was equipped with so many restraints that it made even the slightest movement impossible.) If an inmate was caught talking, he might have been forced to wear the "iron gag"—a piece of metal that was clamped to his tongue while the other end was attached to leather gloves that he had to wear. If he tried to move, it would cause excruciating pain. Several prisoners accidentally cut off their own tongues while wearing the iron gag, and at least one died while being punished with the device.

Another method of torture used at the Eastern State Pen was the water bath. Inmates were tied to the prison walls and sprayed with ice-cold water. Under the most extreme conditions—like in the middle of winter—the water would freeze on the inmates' bodies.

Perhaps the cruelest means of punishing an inmate was to place him in the "Klondike." Other prisons have "The Hole," which is essentially solitary confinement. But the Klondike

was a group of four underground cells without windows or plumbing where inmates were forced to live, often for several weeks at a time.

SWIFT DECLINE AND ABANDONMENT

The Eastern State Penitentiary was designed to change

the prison system in a positive way, but it failed miserably. In fact, when British author Charles Dickens visited the United States in 1842, one of the places that he wanted to see was the Eastern State Pen. From across the Atlantic, Dickens had heard about this unique prison and wanted to see it for himself. He was shocked by what he witnessed there, calling it "hopeless…cruel, and wrong."

Over the years, changes were made in an attempt to remedy the situation, but they didn't help. Finally, in 1971, the penitentiary was officially closed. In the mid-1990s, after sitting abandoned for years, the building was reopened for tours.

"NOT ALL WHO WALK THESE BLOCKS ARE AMONG THE LIVING…"

Looking back at the horrific history of the Eastern State Pen, it should come as no surprise that more than a few ghosts can be found there. In fact, records indicate that inmates reported paranormal activity on the premises as early as the 1940s. Perhaps that explains what happened to locksmith Gary Johnson in the early 1990s, when he was working there during a restoration of the prison. After Johnson opened a door, he saw shadowy shapes moving all around him. It was as if he'd let all the ghosts roam free.

If there's one area of the facility where visitors are most likely to experience paranormal activity, it is Cellblock 12. Many people have reported hearing disembodied voices and laughter and catching glimpses of shadow figures there.

The guard tower that sits high atop the main wall of the penitentiary is also said to be haunted. People standing outside the prison have seen a ghostly figure walking along the wall. It calmly looks down at them from time to time.

"DUDE, RUN!"

Over the years, many ghost-hunting groups have visited the Eastern State Penitentiary. In 2007, *Most Haunted* investigated the place, and *Ghost Adventures* filmed an episode there in 2009. But the Eastern State Pen will forever be remembered for the actions of one of the *Ghost Hunters* crew members during a 2004 investigation.

At approximately 3 A.M., investigator Brian Harnois of The Atlantic Paranormal Society (TAPS) entered Cellblock 4 with crew member Dave Hobbs. As Dave snapped a photograph, he and Brian thought they saw a large black shape rise up and move in front of them. They both panicked, and Brian yelled out the now-famous line, "Dude, run!" Then they bolted down the hallway, much to the chagrin of their fellow investigators (who concluded that the shape was caused by the camera flash). The incident overshadowed an intriguing piece of evidence that was captured later that night, when one of the team's video cameras recorded a dark shape— almost human in form—that appeared to be moving quickly along a cellblock. Try as they might, TAPS was unable to come up with a scientific explanation for the shape, leaving who or what it was open to interpretation.

Get Out of Jail Free

If you would like to potentially encounter a ghost, the Eastern State Pen is open for tours. But be forewarned…a lot of the spirits there are "lifers," and they just might jump at the chance to escape by following you home!

Hauntings at the Winchester Mystery House

Sarah Winchester was an incredibly eccentric woman. She was heir to her husband's rifle fortune, but her fear of ghostly vengeance drove her to build one of the strangest homes ever—the Winchester Mystery House.

The Sad Tale of Sarah Winchester

At age 23, Sarah Lockwood Pardee married William Wirt Winchester, the owner of the Winchester Repeating Arms Company. With its ability to quickly load and fire as many as 15 bullets in rapid succession, the Winchester rifle became a favorite of pioneers as they crossed the ever-expanding United States. As the settlers helped blaze new trails into the nation's frontier, the Winchester rifle protected them from bandits, wild animals, and other dangers in the wilderness. It would come to be known as "the gun that won the West," and it made William Winchester a very wealthy man.

In 1866, William and Sarah had a baby girl they named Annie, but she died when she was only a few weeks old. The baby's death pushed Sarah into a deep depression. When William died in 1881, Sarah was all alone. She inherited her husband's wealth and business, which provided her with an income of more than $1,000 a day.

But money alone can't buy happiness, so the sullen Sarah consulted a medium, who told her that her family was cursed by the souls of those killed by Winchester rifles. When Sarah asked what she could do, she was told that she must move out west and build a house to soothe those spirits. The medium warned Sarah that construction on the house could never end—work must continue around the clock to keep the tormented souls satisfied.

DESIGNED BY SPIRITS

Sarah trekked across the country in 1884 and arrived in San Jose, California, where she purchased a small farm-house and nearly 162 acres of land. Construction began immediately. Instead of using blueprints or plans, Sarah selected an area of the house as her "séance room." Every night between midnight and 2:00 A.M., she would "receive" building instructions from the spirits that haunted the house. In the morning, she would give the workers her own hand-drawn sketches of the work that should be done next.

What an Interesting Place You Have Here

As a result, the house took on some unusual features.
Stained-glass windows gave views of inner walls or closets.
One window was set into the floor. Twisting, turning staircases led back into themselves, or simply nowhere at all. One
set of stairs went straight up to the ceiling. Another had steps
that rose only two inches at a time. Dozens of closets were
installed, ranging in size from that of a three-bedroom
apartment to just one inch deep.

Although Sarah did not entertain visitors, she included two
ballrooms in her constantly growing mansion. The Grand
Ballroom was given rich hardwood flooring, fine oak panels,
and a silver chandelier with 13 candles. One evening, she
threw a lavish dinner party, complete with elegant gold
plates, fine wine, tuxedoed musicians, and dancing far into
the night. However, there was only one attendee—Sarah.

She's Definitely not a Triskaidekaphobe

Sarah was very fond of the number 13. Many of the windows
and doors have 13 panes or panels. A number of staircases
have 13 steps, and some rooms contain 13 windows.
Chandeliers had 13 candles apiece. Many trees planted on
the site are arranged in groups of 13. But not all of Sarah's
eccentricities were over-the-top. At times, she could be
quite inventive. She once created a call box for her servants,
complete with a number system and ringing bells. She even

installed a large oil-burning boiler that fed hot water to a rotating spout on the ceiling of her garage. As a result, Sarah invented the first car wash for the three autos she owned, which were all driven by chauffeurs.

By 1906, the enormous mansion towered seven stories high and had scores of rooms. However, the earthquake that rocked the San Francisco area that year caused the top three floors to collapse. They were never rebuilt, even though construction and remodeling continued around the clock. In fact, the earthquake trapped Sarah for more than an hour under the debris, where she yelled for her servants (and perhaps the spirits of the house) to rescue her.

EVERY GOOD PROJECT HAS AN END... OR DOES IT?

When Sarah Winchester died in 1922, construction had been going nonstop for 38 years. The house sprawled over six acres and boasted 160 rooms, 2,000 doors, 10,000 windows,

47 stairways, 47 fireplaces, 13 bathrooms, and 6 kitchens. It is estimated that more than 500 rooms were actually built and then sealed over or refashioned into new spaces.

Over the years, investigators have recorded many paranormal occurrences at the Winchester Mystery House. One group recorded faint sounds of an organ playing. (Sarah liked to play her pump organ late at night to entertain her spectral guests and exercise her arthritic hands.) They also saw moving balls of light and two apparitions dressed in clothing that was popular in Sarah's time. Other visitors have felt icy chills in draft-free spaces and heard footsteps and breathing in empty rooms. When one guest developed photos he'd taken in the peculiar mansion, he discovered that he'd captured the ghostly image of a man in coveralls. And during a séance in 1975, renowned medium Jeanne Borgen seemed to transform into an elderly Sarah, aging rapidly before the other attendees and falling over in pain.

Many say that the ghost of Sarah Winchester still roams her unusual home, and psychics firmly believe that the house is haunted. This can't be proven, but it doesn't stop the claims— and it didn't stop the lady of the house from undertaking one of the world's most incredible construction projects.

BACHELOR'S GROVE: AMERICA'S MOST HAUNTED CEMETERY?

Bachelor's Grove Cemetery is hidden inside a forest preserve near Midlothian, Illinois. It is thought to be one of the most haunted cemeteries in the United States. Haunted or not, this site certainly has an intriguing past that raises many questions but provides few answers.

ABANDONED AND VANDALIZED

Like almost everything associated with the cemetery, the very origins of Bachelor's Grove are cloaked in mystery. Some claim that the place got its name in the early 1800s when several unmarried men built homes there. Over the years, about 200 individuals made Bachelor's Grove their *final* resting place.

All that changed during the 1960s, when the branch of the highway that ran past the cemetery was closed, cutting the graveyard off from traffic. With the road to it essentially abandoned, people stopped coming to the cemetery. The last burial at Bachelor's Grove took place in 1965.

Due to the cover of the Rubio Woods, the cemetery became a popular location for late-night parties and senseless vandalism. Today, of the nearly 200 graves at the site, only 20 or so still have tombstones. The rest have been broken or stolen. This—combined with rumors that some graves have been dug up—is why many believe that the spirits at Bachelor's Grove do not rest in peace.

GLOW IN THE DARK

Who haunts Bachelor's Grove? For starters, many people have spotted the ghost of a woman dressed in white walking among and sitting on top of the tombstones late at night. She seems unaware of those around her, so it is believed that this is a residual haunting—a replaying of a sad time in her life, perhaps when she would visit the grave of a loved one. In the early 1990s, a paranormal research group claimed to have snapped a photo of her.

People have also reported seeing strange floating orbs of light darting around the cemetery, especially near the pond. Some believe that Chicago-area gangsters dumped the bodies of their victims in the pond and that the lights are the spirits of the dead. Others think that the strange orbs are related to the legend that a man plowing a nearby field died when his horse got spooked and ran into the pond, drowning both itself and the man.  The ghostly farmer and his horse have also been seen from time to time.

Probably the most fascinating paranormal activity reported at Bachelor's Grove is the phantom house. On certain nights, a spectral building is said to appear along the abandoned road leading to the cemetery. Those who have witnessed this strange apparition say that the two-story house slowly fades away until it disappears without a trace. Some people have also spotted a ghostly car—complete with glowing headlights—speeding down the road.

Should you wish to visit Bachelor's Grove in the hopes of encountering some of these spirits, the cemetery is open every day until sunset. Just remember that you are visiting hallowed ground—the final resting place of men, women, and children—so be sure to treat it as such.

THE CLAIRVOYANT CRIME-BUSTER

TV shows like Ghost Whisperer *and* Medium *make the idea of solving crimes through ESP seem almost commonplace. But way before that, there was psychic detective Arthur Price Roberts. His work was accomplished in the early 1900s, when high-tech aids such as DNA identification were still only far-fetched dreams. Police in those times often used psychics to help solve many cases.*

"I SEE DEAD PEOPLE"
Born in Wales in 1866, Arthur Price Roberts moved to Milwaukee, Wisconsin, as a young man. It was there that the man who never learned to read was nicknamed "Doc."

One of his earliest well-known cases involved a baffling missing person incident in Peshtigo, a small town about 160 miles north of Milwaukee. In July 1905, a man named Duncan McGregor had gone missing, leaving no clue as to his whereabouts. The police searched for him for months. Finally McGregor's desperate wife decided to visit the psychic detective who had already made a name for himself in Milwaukee. She didn't even have to explain the situation to Roberts because he knew immediately upon meeting her who she was.

Arthur meditated on the vanished husband, then sadly told Mrs. McGregor that he'd been murdered. He said that Duncan's body was in the Peshtigo River, caught near the bottom in a pile of timber. Arthur proved correct in every detail.

MYSTERY OF THE MAD BOMBERS

Arthur helped solve numerous cases. He helped a Chicago man find his brother who had traveled to New Mexico and had not been heard from for months. Arthur predicted that the brother's body would be found in a certain spot in Devil's Canyon, and it was.

By coming up with new evidence for a last-minute pardon, Arthur saved a Chicago man named Ignatz Potz, who had been sentenced to die for a murder that he didn't commit. But Arthur's most famous feat came in 1935, when he correctly predicted that the city of Milwaukee would be hit by six large dynamite explosions that would destroy a town hall, banks, and police stations. People laughed because such mayhem was unheard of in Milwaukee. Arthur made his prediction on October 18 of that year. About a week later, the Milwaukee area entered a time of terror.

First, a town hall in the suburb of Shorewood was blasted, killing two children and wounding many other people. A few weeks later, the mad bombers hit two banks and two police stations. Federal agents descended upon the city, and several local police officers were assigned to work solely on finding out who was responsible for the bombings. Finally, the police went to Arthur to learn what was coming next. He told them that one more blast was in the works, that it would be south of the Menomonee River, and that it would be the final bomb. Police took him at his word and blanketed the area with officers and sharpshooters.

And sure enough, on November 4, a garage in the area blew to smithereens in an explosion that could be heard as far as eight miles away. The two bombers—young men who were 18 and 21 years old—had been hard at work in the garage assembling 50 pounds of dynamite when their plan literally backfired. Few people argued with Arthur's abilities after that.

HIS FINAL FORTUNE

Arthur's eeriest prediction may have been that of his own death. In November 1939, he told a group of friends that he would be leaving this world on January 2, 1940. And he did, passing quietly in his home on that exact date. Many of his most amazing accomplishments will probably never be known because a lot of his work was done secretly for various law enforcement agencies. But "Doc" Roberts had an undeniable gift, and he died secure in the knowledge that he had used it to help others as best he could.

THE HAUNTED TATTOO PARLOR

When ghost hunters from the Chicago branch of the American Ghost Society first investigated Old Town Tatu in 2006, their goal was to look for ghosts from the days when the building served as a funeral home. But in later investigations, they turned their attention to communicating with more recently departed spirits.

GENERATIONS OF HAUNTINGS

For nearly 75 years, the building that now houses Old Town Tatu on Chicago's north side was the home of the Klemundt Funeral Home. And for years, the Klemundt family had told stories about the building being haunted.

In 2002, the building was purchased for use as a tattoo parlor, and soon after, the new occupants began to experience poltergeist activity and other supernatural phenomena. Decorations fell off the walls as though they were pushed by an unseen force, and small objects flew across the room. One employee even saw an ashtray zip through the air and land upside down without spilling a single ash.

Several employees also witnessed the apparition of a young girl. Some researchers speculated that it was not the ghost of a girl who had died in the building but rather residual energy (sometimes known as a "psychic imprint") from a girl who was terrified when she was left alone in the building years before.

Employees and customers also reported seeing the shadowy specters of a man in a brown suit, a man in a light blue suit, and a woman in a white dress. One employee even heard a disembodied voice in the basement.

Ghosts Exposed

Prior to the American Ghost Society's first investigation of Old Town Tatu in 2006, no one was sure how seriously to take these spooky stories. Veteran ghost hunters are used to people making up tales about women in white and spirits making scary sounds. But they suspected that the tattoo artists weren't making up the stories. After all, the Klemundt family had been telling similar tales for years.

During their search, the researchers found a cold spot in one corner of the basement, and one team member felt something tap him on the shoulder. When an investigator called out "What's your name?," they heard nothing. But later, when reviewing evidence from their audio recorder, they discovered that it had picked up a voice saying the name "Walter."

One theory suggests that this may have been the ghost of Walter Loeding, whose funeral was held in the building in the 1960s. Klemundt family members recalled that Walter didn't own a suit at the time of his death, so they had to buy one in which to bury him. The suit they bought was brown, which is why some believe that Walter is the ghost in a brown suit.

"If I Die in This Place..."

None of this activity seemed to surprise Richie "Tapeworm" Herrera, the owner of the tattoo parlor. Not only did he work in the building, he also lived there. Over the years, he had seen several ghosts, including  "Walter," whom he sometimes caught watching him while he worked at his tattoo station.

"I stopped what I was doing and tried to motion for other people to look," Tapeworm said during the first investigation. "But I wouldn't take my eye[s] off him for one second, man, 'cause I knew that if I looked away for a second, he'd be gone. And he was! The second I looked away, he vanished."

Tapeworm also claimed that ghosts would mess with the appliances in his apartment above the tattoo parlor and would even open the window while he was in the bathroom.

Most of the experiences seemed to amuse Tapeworm more than scare him, but one entity that he encountered on the staircase to his apartment genuinely frightened him.

Having grown up in the neighborhood, Tapeworm had always been fearful of the old tile stairway—the only part of the funeral home that can be seen from the front windows. "I remember being a kid in this neighborhood, and you could see those stairs in the window. I was always all superstitious about it because of what the place was, you know. It was where the dead people were. And now...lo and behold, 30 years later, I'm *living* here. And twice, when I've been walking down those stairs, I felt like something was trying to push me! And that freaks me out because everyone knows you can't fight back with these cats! So the first time it happened, I just looked up and shouted, 'Listen! If I die in this place, it is *on!*'"

The investigators and Tapeworm all shared a hearty laugh. Later, when the researchers reviewed their audio, they found that the sound of ghostly laughter had been recorded on the staircase at the exact moment that a psychic claimed that a spirit thought it was very funny that Tapeworm was afraid of being pushed down the stairs. Tragically, barely three weeks after that initial investigation, Tapeworm had a heart attack in his apartment. He died at age 37, just steps away from the staircase.

You Can't Keep a Good Ghost Down

After Tapeworm's death, his friends and coworkers came to believe that he too was haunting the place. The equipment at Tapeworm's old station would frequently malfunction (or not work at all) when anyone who was not a friend of his tried to use it. In addition, motion-activated cameras recorded unusual blobs that floated up to them and briefly hovered there before drifting away.

A few months after Tapeworm's untimely death, employees were enjoying their annual Halloween party when one of them checked his cell phone and noticed a missed call— from Tapeworm's old number! He called the number the next day and found that it belonged to a confused young woman who had been asleep when the call was made.

One member of the American Ghost Society said that when he returned to the building after Tapeworm's death, he felt as though someone was pulling his hair and flicking his ear—things that a prankster like Tapeworm would do.

Current employees also claim that Tapeworm's ghost seems especially active when they play techno music, which Tapeworm despised. To make his presence (and his dislike of the music) known, Tapeworm likes to make equipment malfunction and cause electrical disturbances. If employees play punk or heavy metal music, which were Tapeworm's favorites, things are much calmer.

Tapeworm has also been known to announce his presence verbally. A psychic who toured the building in 2007 was given no information about the place, yet he said that he sensed the presence of a particularly foul-mouthed spirit. And in 2009, Brad and Barry Klinge from *Ghost Lab* noted a 20-degree temperature drop after calling out, "Hey Richie!" They also picked up an EVP (electronic voice phenomenon) of a voice that Tapeworm's friends identified as his. The voice said a few things that cannot be printed here.

Whether Tapeworm's spirit is actually engaged in an other-worldly battle with the funeral parlor ghosts is unknown. But since his death, his spirit *has* been reported much more often than the others, which leads some to wonder if he kicked their butts so far into oblivion that they're afraid to show up anymore. Those who knew Tapeworm don't doubt it.

RIDDLES OF THE RIDDLE HOUSE

While functioning as a cemetery caretaker's home, the Riddle House in West Palm Beach, Florida, was always close to death. Since then, it's been relocated and repurposed, and now it sees its fair share of life—life after death, that is.

THE "PAINTED LADY"
This pretty "painted lady" (an old Victorian house painted in several cheery colors) was built in 1905 as a cemetery

caretaker's cottage. Cloaked in grand Victorian style, the house exhibited the brightness of life, which seemed out of place next to a cemetery. But perhaps that's what was intended. After all, a cemetery caretaker's duties can be gloomy, so any bit of spirit-lifting would likely be welcomed. Or so its builders thought. In the case of this particular house, the term *spirit-lifting* took on a whole new meaning.

The first specter sighted in the building was that of a former cemetery worker named Buck, who was killed during an argument. Soon after, Buck's ghost was seen doing chores around the cemetery and inside the cottage. Luckily, he seemed more interested in performing his duties than getting revenge.

In the 1920s, the house received its current name when Karl Riddle purchased it and became its caretaker. During his tenure, a grief-stricken employee named Joseph hung himself in the attic. This sparked a frenzy of paranormal phenomena inside the house, including the unexplained sounds of rattling chains and disembodied voices.

After Karl moved out, the reports of paranormal activity slowed down—but the peace and quiet didn't last.

TRAVELING SPIRITS

By 1980, the Riddle House had fallen into disrepair and was abandoned. The city planned to demolish the building but instead decided to give it to Karl's nephew John, who donated it and had it turned into a museum. The entire structure was moved—lock, stock, and barrel—to Yesteryear Village, a museum devoted to Florida's early years. There, it was placed on permanent display as an attractive token of days long past. There, too, its dark side returned...with a vengeance.

When workers began to reassemble the Riddle House, freshly awakened spirits kicked their antics into high gear. Ladders were tipped over, windows were smashed, and tools were thrown to the ground from the building's third floor. Workers were shocked when an unseen force threw a wooden board across a room, striking a carpenter in the head. The attacks were blamed on the spirit of Joseph, and the situation became so dangerous that work on the structure was stalled for six months. After that, the Riddle House was restored to its previous glory.

GHOSTLY UNVEILING

During the dedication of the Riddle House in the early 1980s, two unexpected guests showed up for the ceremony. Grandly dressed in Victorian garb, the couple added an air of authenticity to the celebration. Many assumed they were actors who were hired for the occasion, but they weren't. In fact, no one knew *who* they were. A few weeks later, 100-year-old photographs from the Riddle House were put on display. There in the photos stood the very same couple that guests had seen at the dedication!

When the *Ghost Adventures* team spent a night locked inside the Riddle House in 2008, a medium warned the investigators that the spirit of Joseph is an evil entity that did not want them there. But that didn't stop investigator Zak Bagans from provoking the spirit. Bagans left a board at the top of the stairs and asked the entity to move it if it didn't want them there. Later, after the team heard footsteps in the room above them, the board fell down several stairs on its own. During the night, the team experienced unexplained noises and objects moving and falling by themselves. The researchers concluded that the Riddle House is definitely haunted and that whatever resides in the attic does not like men in particular, just as the medium had cautioned.

Ghostly stirrings at the Riddle House continue to this day. Unexplained sightings of a torso hanging in the attic window represent only part of the horror. And if history is any indicator, more supernatural activity is sure to come.

"It is, alas, chiefly the evil emotions that are able to leave their photographs on surrounding scenes and objects, and whoever heard of a place haunted by a noble deed, or of beautiful and lovely ghosts revisiting the glimpses of the moon?"

—British author Algernon H. Blackwood

Haunted Restaurants

Choosing a place to eat is never simple. What type of food? Formal or informal? And what about spirits? Do you want full apparitions or invisible entities? In many restaurants across America, the question isn't whether to dine with a ghost or be haunt-free, but rather how many ghosts might join the meal.

Country Tavern (Nashua, New Hampshire)

In 1741, a merchant-ship owner known as Captain Ford built a farmhouse for himself and his young wife Elizabeth. His business often took him away from home for long periods of time. After one trip that lasted for about a year, Captain Ford returned home to discover that his wife had recently given birth to a baby girl. Knowing that the child couldn't possibly be his, he locked his wife in a closet and killed the infant. Then he released Elizabeth and stabbed her. Ford buried the baby in the yard and dumped Elizabeth's body in a well.

In the early 1980s, when the Country Tavern opened in the old farmhouse, the ghost of Elizabeth—who had been seen on the grounds of her former abode many times since her death—made herself at home. A blonde woman in a white Colonial-style dress with blue ribbons has been spotted in the quaint restaurant's dining rooms, kitchen, and women's restroom. Elizabeth isn't shy, either. Sometimes she moves plates—occasionally while diners are still eating off them!

She also likes to play with female patrons' hair and tinker with small items. In addition, visitors have noticed her peering through a window in a nearby barn. Elizabeth is the most prominent ghost at the Country Tavern, but people have also heard the faint sound of a baby crying.

ARNAUD'S (NEW ORLEANS, LOUISIANA)

In 1918, Arnaud Casenave—a French wine salesman— opened a restaurant in the heart of New Orleans. It's been a family-owned center of fine dining ever since, but it's not without its ghosts. The specter of a man dressed in an old-fashioned tuxedo is often spotted near the windows of the main dining room. This ghost is believed to be none other than Arnaud himself, still watching over his beloved restaurant. A spectral woman has also been seen walking out of the restroom and moving silently down the hall before disappearing into a wall.

OLD BERMUDA INN (STATEN ISLAND, NEW YORK)

When Martha Mesereau's husband was away fighting in the Civil War, she lit a candle and sat by her bedroom window every night, waiting for his safe return. When she learned that her husband had died in battle, Martha locked herself in her room and died of a broken heart. But she still makes her presence known at her former home, which is now the Old Bermuda Inn—a banquet hall and bed-and-breakfast. Moving cold spots fill the building, and locked doors open on their own. Staff members have also heard Martha crying. When the building was being renovated a few years ago, a painting of Martha spontaneously burst into flames in the hallway. Perhaps she was showing her disapproval of the changes being made to her house. Some diners have seen a woman resembling Martha walking through the dining room, and others have seen her sitting by the window, just like she did in life while waiting for her husband's return.

POOGAN'S PORCH (CHARLESTON, SOUTH CAROLINA)

In 2003, the Travel Channel voted Poogan's Porch the third-most haunted place in America. Staff members and guests have watched a woman in a long black dress disappear in front of their eyes. The same woman has been seen waving from a second-story window. She is believed to be the ghost of Zoe St. Amand, a former schoolteacher who lived in the building until the 1950s.

And then there's the ghost of the restaurant's namesake. Poogan was a stray dog that wandered the neighborhood begging for scraps. While the restaurant was being renovated in the 1970s, he liked to hang out on the porch to watch. The lovable mutt died in 1979, but people relaxing on the porch have felt an animal rub against their legs, even though no creature was there. Not many restaurants can claim a resident ghost dog.

SPIRITS ABOARD THE *QUEEN MARY*

Once one of the world's most magnificent cruise liners, the Queen Mary *played host to rich and famous guests such as Clark Gable, Charlie Chaplin, and Elizabeth Taylor. But in 1967, the stately ship was permanently docked at the Port of Long Beach in California. Since the early 1970s, the* Queen Mary *has been a popular tourist attraction and a luxury hotel.*

What many patrons may not know is that this former grande dame of the sea has a history of paranormal activity, which has been witnessed by passengers and crew members alike. In the early 1980s, Tom Hennessy, a columnist for the *Long Beach Press-Telegram,* decided to check out the alleged hauntings for himself. As a skeptic, Tom didn't expect to find much, but after one rather frightening night aboard the ship, he left a believer.

BIZARRE ACTIVITY

Tom interviewed several people who had worked aboard the *Queen Mary,* and many of them talked openly about their experiences with the ship's ghosts. A security guard told Tom that it wasn't uncommon for lights to mysteriously switch on and off and for doors to slam shut on G Deck, which is where some believe the ship's morgue was located. The guard also described bizarre activity in the ship's artifacts section. There, motion sensors were often set off even though the room was empty and locked up tight.

Other individuals who had worked on the ship told Tom that they'd heard odd clanging noises in the engine room, as if someone was hard at work. But the noises almost always occurred after hours, when the room was unoccupied.

FACE TO FACE WITH GHOSTS

Another security officer revealed to Tom that once, while she was standing on the stairs leading to the swimming pool, she saw a woman in an old-fashioned swimsuit preparing to dive into the empty pool. When the guard yelled to stop her, the woman mysteriously disappeared.

Another time, the same guard was riding the escalator from the engine room when she had the eerie feeling that she was being watched. When she turned around, she saw a man dressed in gray overalls standing behind her. Assuming that the man was a maintenance worker, she stepped aside to let him pass, but he vanished instead.

Other witnesses have also encountered this spectral man in overalls. He has dark hair and a long beard and is believed to have been a mechanic or maintenance worker in the 1930s.

The *Queen Mary* also has its own resident "Lady in White." Who this woman was in life is unknown, but she haunts the Queen's Salon. She wears a long white evening gown, and witnesses say that she dances alone near the grand piano as if listening to music that only she can hear.

Tour guides aboard the *Queen Mary* have also reportedly experienced frightening phenomena, including hearing odd noises and seeing weird lights. One guide said that he heard an unseen man clear his throat, and then he watched as the chain across the entryway to the engine room began to shake violently.

Phantom voices, disembodied footsteps, cold spots, and inexplicable breezes that blow through closed-off areas are some of the other eerie occurrences that take place aboard the *Queen Mary*. While touring the ship, one guest felt someone tugging at her purse, pulling her sweater, and stroking her hair. Cold chills crept down her spine when she realized that no one was near her at the time.

MADE A BELIEVER

Tom Hennessy's personal experience aboard the *Queen Mary* was equally odd. During the half hour he spent alone in the portion of the ship that houses the propeller shafts, the journalist heard weird banging noises that stopped when

he ran toward them and then started again when he walked away. He also reported finding an oil drum blocking an entryway where no oil drum had been before. Later, upon returning to the same passageway, he found two oil drums blocking the way. Tom also experienced rushing air in a supposedly airtight room, mysterious vibrations on a metal catwalk, and the sounds of a nearby conversation—even though the closest crew members were two decks away.

It is natural to assume that the spooks that haunt the *Queen Mary* are former guests and crew members, but their exact identities are unknown. Some speculate that the sounds of rolling metal that are occasionally heard in a particular hatchway may be related to a crewman who was crushed to death there during World War II when the *Queen Mary* was used as a troopship. And odd activity in one kitchen, including disappearing utensils, is believed to be the work of an unpopular cook who was killed during a riot aboard the ship. During the chaos, the cook was allegedly shoved into a hot oven, where he burned to death.

The ghosts of the *Queen Mary* are apparently more into making mischief than mayhem. No one has been hurt or threatened by the spirits, and reports of the ship's paranormal activity have only served to attract more visitors. The *Queen Mary* may no longer be seafaring, but thanks in part to the spirits that remain on board, the ship is as popular as ever.

A Haunting on Chicago's Magnificent Mile

Chicago's Water Tower stands more than 150 feet tall along the world-famous Magnificent Mile. However, many visitors don't realize that the site is haunted by a hero who died there during the Great Chicago Fire of 1871.

Mrs. O'Leary Lit a Lantern in the Shed

On the evening of October 8, 1871, the Great Chicago Fire began behind the O'Leary home. Contrary to popular belief, the fire was not started by a cow kicking over a lantern. Even so, the flames spread quickly from the O'Leary barn.

When the smoke cleared a couple of days later, charred buildings and ashes littered the city. The fire had blazed a path of destruction nearly a mile wide and four miles long, leaving more than 100,000 people homeless. Approximately 300 people died in the fire. One of the dead was a suicide victim who was found inside the Chicago Water Tower.

A Hero's Last Resort?

According to legend, a lone fireman stayed at the water-pumping station in Chicago's Streeterville neighborhood valiantly trying to save as many homes as possible. But as the flames closed in around him, he realized that he was fighting a losing battle and there was nowhere to run.

As the fire edged closer, the brave fireman considered his options. Apparently, a slow death by fire seemed more frightening than a quicker end by his own hand. As the story goes, the fireman climbed the stairs inside the water tower, strung a rope from a beam near the top of the structure, and, in a moment of desperation, looped the rope around his neck and jumped to his death.

THE SOLITARY GHOST

Ironically, the heat of the fire did not destroy the Chicago Water Tower, but it did scorch everything inside. The heroic fireman's identity was never known, but his spirit lingers on. Hundreds of people have seen the sad figure of the hanging man and smelled a hint of smoke inside the tower, often on October nights around the anniversary of the tragedy.

From outside the historic structure, some people see a pale man staring down at them from a window near the top of the tower. His expression is sad and forlorn, and he seems to look right through those on the ground. Other visitors have heard an eerie, sorrowful whistling that seems to come from inside the structure.

However, most people who've seen the Water Tower ghost say he appears with a rope around his neck, swinging and turning slowly. His face is twisted, grotesque, and glowing as if flames are just beneath him. The ghost appears so real that many witnesses have called the police to report a suicide. But responding officers, who have often seen the apparition themselves, know that he's simply a reminder of valor from a tragic fire that occurred more than a century ago.

THREE MEN, A BABY, AND A GHOST

Legend has it that if you pause the comedy hit Three Men and a Baby *in just the right spot, you can see the ghost of a boy who died in the apartment where the movie was filmed. Creepy, but is it true?*

Although there is nothing supernatural about the movie *Three Men and a Baby*, rumors persist that it was the first to capture an actual ghost on film. As with similar movie myths, the rumor about *Three Men and a Baby* began when the film was released on home video. In one scene, Ted Danson's character (Jack) paces around the apartment he shares with his two roommates. Pause the video at the right moment, and in the background of the shot you'll see the ghostly image of a boy in a window. Pause it at a later point in the scene, and the boy has been replaced by the image of what looks like a rifle. According to rumors, a nine-year-old boy killed himself with a shotgun in the apartment before it was used as a set in the movie.

Fortunately, the real explanation is much less sinister. First, the interior scenes of the movie were shot on a set that was built on a soundstage, so there was no actual apartment. In the movie, Jack is an actor, and an earlier scene features a cardboard cutout of him, which served as a prop in a film in which he had recently starred. If you look carefully at the "ghost boy" and the alleged rifle, you'll see that they are simply different shots of that cutout.

Haunted Hospitals Have Tales to Tell

If they could speak, hospitals would have incredible stories to tell. Within their walls, lives are saved and lives are lost. People undergo surgeries and heal from injuries—but some never leave. Doctors and nurses have personal dramas and patients have near-death experiences, so it's not surprising that hospitals are among the most haunted places you'll find.

Carrie Tingley Children's Hospital (Albuquerque, New Mexico)

Originally established in the city of Truth or Consequences, New Mexico, Carrie Tingley Children's Hospital was founded in 1937 to help kids suffering from polio. It was later moved to Albuquerque. Some unused areas of the hospital are said to have invisible force fields that sometimes prevent people from moving through certain hallways or doors. Employees know to listen for a hissing sound that is heard just before a barrier is encountered. Glowing rooms, disembodied voices, and phantom heartbeats and sobbing are all part of the haunting there.

DOCTORS HOSPITAL (PERRY HEIGHTS, OHIO)

You'd expect former patients to haunt a hospital, but the ghost of a former nurse's aide also wanders Doctors Hospital, humming just the way she used to in life. An elderly woman who died there also reportedly haunts the room in which she passed. After her death in the late 20th century, patients felt cold spots in the room and even had their blankets pulled off them. The room was eventually sealed off and was no longer in use when the hospital closed its doors in 2008.

In March 2010, the Ohio Exploration Society—a group of paranormal researchers—visited the hospital. They tried to record EVPs (electronic voice phenomena) in the woman's room without success, but that doesn't mean all was quiet— the investigators did capture an unexplained voice in the hospital lab.

LINDA VISTA COMMUNITY HOSPITAL (LOS ANGELES, CALIFORNIA)

A hospital with too many unexplained deaths sounds like the perfect place to find a ghost or two. Linda Vista, which was built in 1904, is now closed and is said to be haunted by both patients and staff. Elevators start and stop by themselves;

a green light glows faintly throughout the night and other lights flicker on and off; moans and screams have been heard; the image of a doctor has been observed in an upper-story window; and on the third floor, unexplained foul odors are often detected. Visitors also report seeing a spectral girl playing outside and hearing her laugh.

MADISON CIVIL WAR HOSPITAL (MADISON, GEORGIA)

When the Madison Civil War Hospital served as a military medical facility, it certainly saw its share of sick and injured soldiers...and death. Although it's no longer in use, the building still has some life in it—afterlife, that is. Paranormal investigators have heard phantom footsteps in an empty stairwell and rustling sounds in a seemingly unoccupied basement. They've also seen a ball bouncing down a hallway by itself. In addition, ghost hunters have witnessed a number of strange specters there, including a man dressed in black who was spotted at the top of the stairs and a woman in a blue gown who lingers in one particular room.

"The oldest and strongest emotion of mankind is fear, and the oldest and strongest kind of fear is fear of the unknown."

—H. P. Lovecraft

FRIGHTENING FACTS

- *For many years, the Martha Washington Hotel in Manhattan was a female-only residence, so it's not surprising that the building's resident ghost is a crabby elderly lady. This eternal tenant seems to resent intruders—so much so that she likes to hold pillows over their faces while they sleep.*

- *"The Unsinkable" Molly Brown, a Titanic survivor and socialite, lived in Denver for years. The spunky woman's spirit remains in her beloved former home, which is now a museum that showcases her life and offers exhibits about Victorian-era culture. Her apparition has been spotted there wearing old-fashioned attire. She also likes to open and close doors.*

- *Johnny Appleseed was a real person named John Chapman, and his "legend" is actually quite factual. His family's cemetery is located near Dexter City, Ohio, and Johnny's big-hearted specter likes to visit there often. Look for a barefoot man in tattered clothes.*

- *Most of the paranormal activity at Alcatraz—America's most infamous prison—takes place in Cells 11D through 14D. There, visitors often hear disembodied voices, experience a profound sense of sorrow, and feel icy, cold temperatures.*

The Lemp Mansion:
A Favorite Haunt in St. Louis

Over the course of several generations, the Lemp family experienced enormous success and horrific tragedies. Fortunes were made and lives were destroyed, and much of the misfortune took place in the Lemp Mansion. In recent years, the house has been listed on several "most haunted" lists. It is open to the public as a restaurant and bed-and-breakfast, catering mainly to those who love a good ghost story.

Pursuing the American Dream

Adam Lemp left Germany in 1836 to pursue the American Dream. By 1838, he had settled in St. Louis, Missouri, where he opened a grocery store that sold his own special homemade beer. By 1840, Adam's beer was so popular that he started his own brewery. By the time he died in 1862, he was a self-made millionaire.

When Adam died, his son William inherited the brewery and his father's wealth. William built up the brewery and was perhaps the Lemp Mansion's first ghost.

The Tragedies Begin

In 1868, William's father-in-law built the house that would come to be known as the Lemp Mansion. William bought the house from him in 1876, and he spared no expense in making it his own, expanding it to 33 rooms and adding an underground tunnel that connected the house to the brewery, which was located just a couple blocks away.

Although William had four sons, he hoped that his beloved son Frederick would one day take over the family business. Frederick was hardworking and ambitious, but he may have worked himself too hard because in 1901, he died of heart failure at age 28.

William was never quite the same after Frederick's death. He kept to himself and lost interest in the brewery, and his health began to decline. Finally, just after breakfast on the morning of February 13, 1904, William's suffering became unbearable. He went to his bedroom and shot himself in the head. No suicide note was ever found.

Where There's a Will, There's a Way
William Lemp Jr. succeeded his father as president of the brewery. Will Jr. and his wife Lillian spent their money on extravagant things. Lillian, who was partial to all things lavender, became known as the "Lavender Lady." The couple had a son, William III, and all seemed right with their world.

But in 1911, Will Jr. and Lillian divorced, and the Lavender Lady went into seclusion.

Following in Father's Footsteps
In the early 20th century, several small, independent brewers combined into one large company, which created competition

and a decline in sales for the Lemp Brewing Company. But the 1919 passage of the 18th Amendment—which kicked off the Prohibition era by making the manufacture, transport, and sale of alcohol illegal in the United States—proved to be the final nail in the coffin for the Lemp Brewing Company, which simply closed down for good one morning.

Fortunately for the Lemps, the beer business had been good to them, and they were financially secure. But money can't buy happiness, and that was certainly true for the Lemps. On March 20, 1920, Will Jr.'s sister Elsa shot herself. Just like her father, she did not leave a suicide note.

The death of his sister and the loss of the family business proved to be more than Will Jr. could handle. Like his father, he became depressed and withdrawn. On December 29, 1922, he was found dead in his office. He had shot himself in the chest.

With Will Jr. gone and his brothers Charles and Edwin involved in their own pursuits, it seemed that the days of the Lemp empire had come to an end. But the specter of tragedy had not left the family just yet.

After Will Jr.'s death, Charles, a lifelong bachelor, moved into the mansion. He remodeled the home and hired two live-in servants for company. By age 77, Charles was an eccentric recluse. Because of the history of the place, his brother

Edwin encouraged him to move out of the house, but Charles had developed a morbid attachment to the family home and refused to leave.

Instead, Charles became the fourth member of the Lemp family to take his own life in the mansion. Sometime during the early morning hours of May 10, 1949, he went to the basement and shot his beloved dog. Then he went upstairs to his second-floor bedroom and shot himself. He was the only member of the Lemp family to leave a suicide note, in which he wrote, "In case I am found dead, blame it on no one but me."

The Ghosts Come Out

The Lemp family, once so large and prosperous, had been nearly destroyed in less than 50 years. Only Edwin Lemp remained, and for years, he had shunned the family business and the home that had been the site of so much tragedy for his family. In 1970, at age 90, he died of natural causes at his secluded estate, Cragwold.

After the death of Charles Lemp, the mansion was sold and turned into a boarding house but with little success. The neighborhood declined and the mansion fell into disrepair. That's when the ghosts came out. The eerie sounds of unexplainable knocks and phantom footsteps sent residents running, and new ones were hard to find.

In 1975, Dick Pointer and his family bought the Lemp Mansion and made it into a restaurant and bed-and-breakfast.

The Pointers undertook a massive renovation to restore the Victorian beauty of the old house and honor its history.

That history has certainly made itself known. During the restoration, workers reported many strange incidents. Cold spots, feelings of being watched, odd noises, and missing tools were enough to make more than one worker bolt.

But the Pointers embrace the ghosts. People come to see the mansion in all its splendor, and the spirits do not disappoint. The Lemp Mansion has been named one of the ten most haunted houses in America, one of *Life* magazine's ten most haunted places, and Missouri's most haunted house.

Staff members and guests alike report brushes with the paranormal there. Items are rearranged, cell phones disappear or ring when no one is on the other end, lights turn on and off by themselves, and doors lock and unlock on their own. Inexplicable sounds and the smell of lavender have also been noted. Visitors have watched as glasses fly though the air, chairs move on their own, and candles ignite by themselves.

Ghostly apparitions have also been spotted. A face has been seen looking out from a room in the attic; Charles Lemp and his phantom pooch have been witnessed; and the Lavender Lady has made spectral appearances as well. One guest awoke to see the ghost of a woman standing next to her bed. The phantom raised a finger to her lips, as if asking the sleepy guest not to scream, and then she quickly vanished.

In a 2010 episode of the TV show *Ghost Hunters*, Jason Hawes and Grant Wilson spent the night at the Lemp Mansion to explore claims of paranormal activity. The investigators witnessed the lights of a K-2 meter (which is used to detect changes in electromagnetic fields) flashing in response to their questions. And then there was the word game. The researchers split up and went to separate rooms, then Jason uttered a single word to the spirits and asked them to say that word to Grant. In his room, Grant heard the word whispered in his ear. Whether this was a trick, the power of suggestion, or the real deal may never be known. But at the end of the visit, Jason was ready to declare the house haunted. Grant wasn't so sure, but he did admit that something weird was going on there.

The Pointer family accepts these resident ghosts as part of the character and charm of the historic house, which attracts many visitors hoping to have paranormal encounters. As Paul Pointer (Dick's son) once said, "Fortunately for us, they are rarely disappointed."

THERE'S SOMETHING ABOUT MARY

Most big cities have their share of ghost stories, and Chicago is no exception. But beyond tales of haunted houses, spirit-infested graveyards, and phantom-filled theaters, one Chicago legend stands out among the rest. It's the story of a beautiful vanishing hitchhiker that nearly everyone in the Windy City has heard about. Her name is "Resurrection Mary," and she is Chicago's most famous ghost.

One version of the story says that Resurrection Mary was a young woman who died on Archer Avenue in Chicago's south-western suburbs. On a cold winter's night in the early 1930s, Mary spent the evening dancing with her boyfriend at the Oh Henry Ballroom (known today as Willowbrook Ballroom) in Willow Springs. But after the two lovers had an argument, Mary decided to walk home. Tragically, she was killed when a passing car slid on the ice and struck her.

Mary's grieving parents buried her in Resurrection Cemetery, just down the road from the ballroom. She was reportedly wearing a fine white dress and dancing shoes when she was laid to rest.

THE GIRL BY THE SIDE OF THE ROAD

Since that time, drivers have often witnessed a ghostly young woman standing on the side of the road near the gates of Resurrection Cemetery. Time and time again, motorists have reported picking up a pretty hitchhiker on Archer Avenue, only to have her disappear before they could drop her off. These accounts feature eerie similarities. In most cases, the woman is said to have blonde hair and wear a white party dress. The encounters almost always occur near the ballroom or in the vicinity of Resurrection Cemetery.

Other reports took a more mysterious turn. Many young men claimed that they'd met a girl at a dance at the ballroom, spent the evening with her, and then offered her a ride home at closing time. Her vague directions always led them north along Archer Avenue until they reached the gates of Resurrection Cemetery—where the girl would inexplicably vanish from the car.

Although some drivers claimed that the mysterious woman was looking for a ride, others reported that she actually tried to jump onto the running boards of their automobiles as they drove past. And some even said that they'd accidentally hit her outside the cemetery. When they went to her aid, her body was gone. Others said that their automobiles actually drove through the young woman before she disappeared through the cemetery gates.

Police and local newspapers fielded similar stories from numerous frightened and frazzled drivers who had encountered the ethereal young woman. These accounts created the legend of "Resurrection Mary," as the mysterious hitchhiker came to be known.

JERRY'S TALE

No Resurrection Mary story is as detailed or as frightening as that of Jerry Palus, who claimed that he met her at a Chicago dance hall in 1939. According to Palus, the pair shared many spins around the dance floor before the young woman asked him for a ride home. She asked him to take Archer Avenue, which he knew was nowhere near the home address she had given him. Nevertheless, he complied. When the car approached Resurrection Cemetery, the young woman asked Palus to pull over. He didn't understand why she wanted to be dropped off in such a remote area. "This is where I have to get out," she explained in a soft voice, "but where I'm going, you can't follow." With that, the mysterious girl hurried toward the cemetery gates and vanished right before Palus's unbelieving eyes.

The next day, Palus visited the home address that the girl had given him. There, an older woman explained to him that he couldn't possibly have been with her daughter because she had been dead for several years. When Palus was shown a photo of the woman's daughter, his face turned pale as he realized that somehow, the young woman had come back from the grave to dance once again.

WILL THE REAL RESURRECTION MARY PLEASE STAND UP?

Told countless times over the years, this legend may actually have some elements of truth to it—but there might be more than one Resurrection Mary haunting Archer Avenue.

It is possible that in life, Resurrection Mary was a young Polish girl named Mary Bregovy. Mary loved to dance, especially at the Oh Henry Ballroom. She was killed one night in March 1934 after spending the evening there and then at some of Chicago's late-night clubs. She died when the car in which she was riding collided with an elevated train support downtown. Soon after Bregovy was buried in Resurrection Cemetery, a caretaker spotted her ghost walking through the graveyard. Stranger still, motorists on Archer Avenue soon began telling stories of seeing her apparition trying to hitch rides as they passed the cemetery. For this reason, many believe that the ghost stories about Mary Bregovy may have given birth to the legend of Resurrection Mary.

However, descriptions of the spectral girl have varied over the years. Mary Bregovy had bobbed light-brown hair, but most reports describe Resurrection Mary as having long blonde hair. So who could this ghost be?

Perhaps it's Mary Miskowski, who was killed along Archer Avenue in October 1930. She also loved to dance at the Oh Henry Ballroom and at some other local nightspots. Many people who knew her in life believed that she might be the ghostly hitchhiker spotted in the southwest suburbs.

We may never know Resurrection Mary's true identity, but there's no denying that sightings of her have been backed up with credible eyewitness accounts. Witnesses have given

specific places, dates, and times for their run-ins with
Mary—encounters that remain unexplained to this day.
Mary is also one of the few ghosts that's left physical
evidence behind.

BURNING DESIRE

Over the years, encounters with Resurrection Mary have
been relatively common, but one account stands apart from
the rest. On August 10, 1976, a man driving past Resurrection
Cemetery noticed a woman in a white dress standing inside
the gates. She was grasping the metal bars of the gate, looking
out toward the road. Thinking
that she had been locked in,
the driver notified the police.
An officer responded to the
call, but when he arrived at
the cemetery, the girl was
gone. He searched the grounds
but found nothing out of the
ordinary—until he glanced at
the gate. It looked as though
someone had yanked two of the bars with such intensity that
small handprints were scorched into the metal.

When word about the handprints got out, people from all
over the area came to see them. Cemetery officials denied
that anything supernatural had occurred, and they later
claimed that the marks were created when a workman had

tried to heat up the bars and bend them back into shape after a truck accidentally drove into the gate. It was certainly a convenient explanation, but one that failed to account for the indentations that appeared to have been left by small fingers and were plainly visible in the metal.

Cemetery officials were disturbed by this new publicity, so in an attempt to dispel the crowds of curiosity seekers, they tried to remove the marks with a blowtorch. However, this process made them even more noticeable, so the officials had the bars cut out and planned to straighten or replace them. But removing the bars only made things worse, as people wondered what the cemetery was trying to hide. So the bars were put back into place, straightened, and then left alone so that the burned areas would oxidize and eventually resemble the other bars. But the blackened areas didn't oxidize, and the twisted handprints remained visible until the late 1990s, when the bars were finally removed. At great expense, Resurrection Cemetery replaced its front gates, and the notorious bars were gone for good.

A Broken Spirit Lingers On

Sightings of Resurrection Mary aren't as frequent now as in years past, but they still persist, and some of them seem to be authentic. Many believe that Mary is on her way to her eternal resting place after one last night of dancing.

NOTABLE ATTEMPTS TO PROVE THE EXISTENCE OF AN AFTERLIFE

When you're investigating the afterlife, ridicule from skeptics comes with the territory. But for many researchers, inventors, and weekend mad scientists, the potential payoff of proving that there's life after death is well worth any taunting. Here are some noteworthy pursuits of prodding into the great hereafter.

- In 1901, surgeon Duncan MacDougall attempted to weigh the human soul. He laid dying tuberculosis patients on massive scales and noted any changes at the moment of death. Based on six weigh-ins, he determined that body weight drops about ¾ ounce (21 grams) when a person dies— presumably because the immortal soul exits the premises.

- In the 1920s, two Dutch physicists claimed that, during a séance, a spirit had explained to them how to build a soul-detecting machine. The spirit said the human soul lives on as a gaseous body, which could interact with the physical world by expanding and contracting. The physicists built an elaborate pressure detector and reported that the entity they encountered did indeed alter gas pressure.

- In order to stop fake mediums from capitalizing on his fame after he died, renowned escape artist and psychic debunker Harry Houdini vowed that if he could communicate from beyond the grave, he would relay a ten-word code that was known only to his wife. For ten years, Houdini's wife held séances on the anniversary of his death (Halloween), but the code never came through.

- At the time of his death in 1931, Thomas Edison was reportedly working on a type of megaphone that would allow, in his words, "personalities which have left this earth to communicate with us." However, no one has ever uncovered any "Spirit Phone" prototypes or technical specs.

- In the 1960s and '70s, Latvian scientist Konstantin Raudive recorded 70,000 EVPs (electronic voice phenomena), which he believed were ghostly voices captured on audiotape.

- In the 1970s, two scientists in Iceland spent four years compiling accounts from a thousand doctors and nurses of what their patients experienced as they approached death. The researchers noted persistent common details in the reports, which covered the experiences of people of all ages with highly varied cultural backgrounds. The most common themes were a bright light, an overpowering feeling of peace, and a sense of an otherworldly realm.

- In 2000, Oregon rancher Lewis Hollander Jr. tried his hand at soul weighing. He enlisted eight sheep, three lambs, and a goat as his subjects. (The animals were already at death's door.) No animals lost weight as they passed on. In fact, all of the sheep *gained* weight for one to six seconds after death. One sheep put on almost two pounds!

• In order to test the validity of reports of near-death, out-of-body experiences, psychiatry professor Bruce Greyson displays distinctive images while patients undergoing heart-related testing are briefly brain dead. So far, no one has recalled seeing the pictures.

• In 2008, English physician Sam Parnia launched a similar experiment that was designed to test the validity of out-of-body experiences in heart attack survivors. He outfitted an operating room with shelves showing pictures that were only visible from the top of the room. His goal was to analyze the near-death recollections of 1,500 patients. Based on his results, he concluded that the human mind (or brain) continues to function during the earliest stages of death.

"Some people believe that when you die there is a wonderful light. As bright as the sun but it doesn't hurt to look into it. All the answers to all the questions you want to know are inside that light. And when you walk to it . . . you become a part of it forever."

—Dr. Lesh (Beatrice Straight's character in *Poltergeist*)

If These Walls Could Talk...
Oh, Wait, They Do Talk!

There are few haunted places featured in more publications and on more television shows than the Whispers Estate, which is considered one of the most haunted places in Indiana. This 3,700-square-foot Victorian mansion in the town of Mitchell has attracted tourists, ghost hunters, psychics, the media, and, of course, ghosts galore.

When Dr. John Gibbons and his wife, Jessie, moved into their dream house in 1899, they had no idea that it would one day become famous for incredibly unusual reasons. The childless couple adopted three orphans, but tragedy surrounded the family. Their oldest daughter, Rachael, set a fire in the house, severely burning herself in the process. She died in an upstairs bedroom two days later. Soon after, her spirit began showing itself to the living. Her apparition is often seen roaming around the estate, and burn marks are still visible in the parlor where the fire started.

The Gibbons family suffered another tragedy when their adopted daughter Elizabeth died of unknown causes at age 10 months. She passed away in the master bedroom. Many people who have stayed in this room have reportedly smelled baby powder lingering in the air. Some have also heard the soft sound of a baby crying.

Due to yet another misfortune that befell this family, the master bedroom has been the site of other ghostly activity. After the deaths of two of her children, Mrs. Gibbons contracted pneumonia and died there as well. In addition to the sound of a baby nearby, visitors to this room have heard noises that resemble ragged breathing and coughing—like someone with pneumonia. Some have even felt pressure on their chests. Other odd occurrences have also been observed there, including a closet door that opens suddenly and door-knobs that jiggle by themselves.

A GATHERING OF GHOSTS

Old houses often have rich histories, but the Whispers Estate has witnessed more sadness than most. In the building's early years, Dr. Gibbons ran his practice on the main level of the house, and it is quite likely that several of his patients died there. Then, in 1966, a man died of a heart attack in the house. And in 1974, his nine-year-old son—who suffered from hydrocephalus (water on the brain)—fell down a flight of stairs and passed away before help could arrive.

In addition to the house, which seems to have produced quite a few ghosts of its own, four graves and an area called the "pit grave" are located on the property. In the pit grave, Dr. Gibbons disposed of the by-products of his

medical practice, such as amputated limbs and organs that he had removed.

While there is no evidence of illegal or immoral activity on the property, psychics who have investigated the Whispers Estate without knowing its history sensed that sinister things happened there. They all felt that the doctor may have been involved in unethical practices. There's nothing like a little dark energy to contribute to a place's paranormal activity.

It's Hard to Sleep with All That Whispering

In 2006, the building was turned into a bed-and-breakfast. But apparently, the spirits of those who once lived there objected to the idea, so they came out in full force. Guests at the B & B have reported hearing whispering throughout the entire mansion. It is difficult to pinpoint the source of these voices, but those hearing them—and there are many—all describe the same type of muffled noises. That's how the place became known as the Whispers Estate. Unfortunately, the building's reputation proved to be bad for business.

However, word about the house spread among those inter- ested in the paranormal, and the Whispers Estate has since become a popular destination for ghost hunters and reporters who come to document the terrifying tales.

One supernatural entity at the inn that doesn't seem to be connected to any one person or event is an apparition or shadow figure that's been dubbed "Big Black." Big Black has been viewed most often in the doctor's quarters, but it has occasionally been seen in other areas of the building as well. Investigators agree that this entity is "not of this world."

In addition, guests who've stayed at the bed-and-breakfast have reported feeling intense tremors while in the doctor's bathroom. And in the master bedroom, many have seen the beds shake violently. Women, especially, have felt the sensation that Dr. Gibbons is whispering in their ears, and some have reported feeling that his ghost actually touched them.

Sensory Scent-sations

Unexplained smells commonly occur in haunted places, and the Whispers Estate is no exception. In addition to the smell of baby powder, many visitors have caught whiffs of cologne, cigars, and the repulsive odor of used bandages.

Paranormal investigators who have studied the Whispers Estate have experienced many unusual phenomena, but one that has been noted over and over is associated with the door in the servants' quarters. When investigators leave that area, the heavy wooden door often mysteriously slams shut behind them with tremendous force. This may be the ghostly version of the phrase, "Here's your hat; what's your hurry?" After all, the ghostly whispers never seem to say, "Please stay."

HERE LIE THE GHOSTS OF PRISONERS PAST

*There's something about a prison that's a little scary...
to most of us, anyway. But add the elements of murder,
brutal assault, suicide, and riots, and you have an
atmosphere that's perfect for paranormal activity. Society
wanted these hardened criminals to remain behind
bars for life, but some are bound there for eternity.*

BURLINGTON PRISON (MOUNT HOLLY, NEW JERSEY)

When it was built in 1811, the Burlington Prison was
designed to house just 40 convicts. But like most other
prisons, it eventually became overcrowded. When it closed
in 1965, nearly 100 inmates were confined there.

The prison is now a museum, but many of the former
inmates are still there to welcome visitors—at least in spirit.
When remodeling began in 1999, ghosts started making
their presence known. Not surprisingly, workers weren't
too thrilled to be sharing the building with the spirits of
the dead, so paranormal experts were called in to put their
fears to rest. Unfortunately, that strategy backfired when the
ghost hunters declared the place to be haunted. Some of the
unexplained activity included missing tools showing up in
different locations, unusual noises, and two apparitions—one
in the shower area and another that is thought to have been a
prisoner who hung himself in a maximum-security cell.

IDAHO STATE PENITENTIARY (BOISE, IDAHO)

When the Idaho State Penitentiary opened around 1870, its first crop of inmates were model prisoners. But by the 1930s, the convicts brought there were much more violent and cunning. The prison closed in the 1970s due to riots brought on by the prison's pitiful living conditions. And where there is violence, there's also a good chance that spirits will linger behind. It's no surprise that a tremendous feeling of sadness is often experienced in the execution chamber. Some visitors have become agitated and overcome with a feeling of dread, while others have broken down in tears or felt physically ill. And then there are the noises—crying, moaning, and the sounds of guards walking the halls radiate from this facility's walls. The prison is now a museum and is open for public tours. So if you're in the area, stop by for a visit—if you dare!

OLD CITY JAIL (CHARLESTON, SOUTH CAROLINA)

Before Charleston's city jail was built in 1802, the land on which it stands was designated for public use. Runaway slaves were held at a workhouse there, and the homeless came by for free meals and medical care. After the jail was built, the hardened convicts and the criminally insane moved in. Over the years, the facility held pirates of the high seas and a number of slaves who were involved in a revolt in 1822. With its long history and unusual combination of residents, it's no surprise that the Old City Jail has more than a few ghosts hanging around.

One of the specters that's frequently observed at the jail is probably a slave from the days when the site was a workhouse. His clothing is ragged and he appears to be carrying a heavy load on his shoulders. He seems unaware of the living. A more violent presence also resides at the jail. Some visitors have experienced the sensation that they were being pushed, tugged, or tapped by an unseen force, and many have even felt physically ill. Today, the Old City Jail building houses the American College of the Building Arts.

SOUTHERN OHIO CORRECTIONAL FACILITY (LUCASVILLE, OHIO)

One of the worst prison riots in history took place in April 1993 at the Southern Ohio Correctional Facility. For ten days, some 450 prisoners staged an uprising in Cellblock L of this maximum-security prison. In the end, five prisoners were sentenced to death for their roles in the violence, which left nine prisoners and one guard dead. Since then, guards patrolling Cellblock L have reported seeing apparitions in the area. They've also heard doors slam and seen shadows when no one else was around. One guard followed a prisoner who was walking the halls after lockdown, only to watch the man vanish before his very eyes.

THE GHOSTS OF SEATTLE'S PIKE PLACE MARKET

Each year, millions of people visit Seattle's Pike Place Market, which is known for a store where employees toss fish at each other at a dizzying pace. As it turns out, the living aren't the only ones attracted to the market.

WHERE SHOPPING CAN BE A SPIRITUAL EXPERIENCE

Pike Place Market, which opened in August 1907, is one of the oldest farmers' markets in the United States. On its first day of business, more than 10,000 shoppers flocked to the eight farmers who had brought their goods to Seattle's waterfront. The market really took off later that year when the first permanent building was constructed at the site.

One of the market's most frequent phantom visitors is Princess Angeline, the daughter of Chief Seattle—a leader of the tribes that lived in the area before the arrival of white settlers. By the late 1850s, many Native Americans had left the area due to the terms of a treaty between the tribes and the U.S. government. But Angeline stayed in Seattle and was a familiar figure along the waterfront. She became something of a local celebrity.

Angeline died in 1896 at age 85. So when Pike Place Market was built on the site of her former home, it was like sending out an open invitation for her to hang around for a while.

And Angeline has apparently accepted the offer. Her ghost has been spotted at many different locations in the market, but she seems particularly fond of a wooden column on the lower level. Abnormally cold air is said to surround this column, and photographs of it reputedly show things that aren't apparent to the naked eye.

With her braided gray hair, slow way of moving, and habit of browsing, Angeline's apparition easily passes for an elderly shopper. She has often fooled people, who react to her as if she's a fellow shopper—until she startles them by vanishing right before their eyes. Sometimes, Angeline's ghost even treats folks to a light show, changing from a glowing white figure to blue, lavender, or pink.

You're Never Alone at Pike Place Market

While Angeline does her best to make as many ghostly appearances at the market as possible, she's not the only spectral spectacle at Pike Place. Workers have heard disembodied lullabies drifting through the air late at night after the market is closed. It is said that they come from the ghost of a heavy-set female barber who used to softly sing her customers to sleep and then pick their pockets while they snoozed. Unfortunately, she was not as good at walking as she was at singing, and one day, she fell through a weak floor to her death. Her ethereal song continues to this day, which seems to contradict the saying, "It ain't over until the fat lady sings."

Another spirit that calls Pike Place home is Arthur Goodwin, the market's director from 1918 to 1941. Ever the workaholic, Arthur's shadowy figure can often be seen looking down at the market from his former office on the upper floor, still keeping an eye on business.

A small spectral boy has also been seen in a craft shop that sells beads. He's been known to open and shut the cash register and tug at sleeves to get attention. At one point during renovations to the store, a small stash of beads was discovered in a wall. It's believed that the ghostly boy was hiding beads there to play with later, as kids often do.

A Specter with a Sweet Tooth

Some angry spirits have been heard arguing inside the walk-in freezer of a deli. A few deli employees simply refuse to go into the freezer because they're afraid of being drawn into whatever dispute these ghosts have with each other.

Other ghostly goings-on occur in a bookstore, where employees sometimes hear footsteps echoing through the aisles, even though they're the only ones in the store. And proving that even a ghost can have a sweet tooth, a candy store at the market has its own resident ghost. On several occasions, employees have put the candy scoops away at night, only to find them back out the next morning.

THE GHOSTS OF ANTIETAM

With nearly 23,000 soldiers wounded or killed, the Battle of Antietam was one of the bloodiest single-day skirmishes of the American Civil War. More than 3,600 of those men died suddenly and violently that day—ripped out of this world and sent reeling into the next. It's no wonder that the ghosts of some of those soldiers still haunt the Antietam battlefield in western Maryland. Perhaps they're still trying to understand what happened to them on that terrible day.

GAELIC GHOSTS

Bloody Lane at Antietam National Battlefield is a sunken road that's so named because of the incredible slaughter that took place there on September 17, 1862. One of the battalions that fought at Bloody Lane was the Union's Irish Brigade, which lost more than 60 percent of its soldiers that day. The brigade's war cry was *faugh-a-ballaugh* (pronounced "fah-ah-bah-LAH"), which means "clear the way" in Gaelic.

Many years ago, a group of schoolchildren took a class trip to Antietam. After touring the battlefield, several boys walked down Bloody Lane toward an observation tower that had been built where the Irish Brigade had charged into battle. Later, back at the school, the boys wrote that they heard odd noises coming from a nearby field. Some said that it sounded like a chant. Others likened the sounds to the "fa-la-la-la-la" portion of the Christmas carol "Deck the Halls." Did the boys hear the ghostly battle cry of the Irish Brigade?

On another occasion, some battle reenactors were lying on the ground near the sunken road when they suddenly began hearing a noise that they were very familiar with—the sound of a regiment marching in full battle gear. Their experience as reenactors allowed them to pick out specific sounds, such as knapsacks, canteens, and cartridge boxes rattling and scraping. But no matter how hard they looked, the men could find no marching soldiers. They concluded that the sounds were made by an otherworldly regiment.

PRYING EYES

Because of its strategic location on the battlefield, the Phillip Pry House was pressed into service as a makeshift hospital during the battle. Much misery took place there, including the death of Union General Israel B. Richardson, despite the loving care of his wife Frances. In 1976, the house was damaged by fire. One day during the restoration, the wife of a park ranger saw a woman dressed in Civil War–era attire coming down the stairs. She asked her husband who the woman was, but he had no knowledge of a woman wearing such clothes at the park.

Later, a woman was seen staring out an upstairs window in the room where General Richardson died. Nothing was particularly unusual about this—except that the room was being renovated at the time and didn't have a floor! Was it the ghost of Frances Richardson, still trying to take care of her dying husband?

Members of the construction crew that was working at the house abandoned the project immediately after sighting this female phantom. Disembodied footsteps have also been heard going up and down the home's stairs.

SCREAMING SPECTERS

The spirits of Antietam are not just confined to the battle-field. Injured Confederate soldiers were brought to St. Paul Episcopal Church in Sharpsburg, and sometimes the sounds of the wounded screaming in agony can still be heard there. Mysterious lights have also been seen in the church's tower.

A BRIDGE BETWEEN TWO WORLDS

Burnside Bridge was another scene of massive slaughter at Antietam, as Union troops repeatedly tried to take the tiny stone span, only to be driven back by intense Confederate fire. Many of the soldiers who died there were quickly buried in unmarked graves near the bridge. Now it seems that arrangement wasn't to their liking. Many credible witnesses, including park rangers, have reported seeing blue balls of light floating near the bridge at night. The faint sound of a phantom drumbeat has also been heard in the vicinity.

Although the Battle of Antietam took place more than 150 years ago, it seems that in some places, the battle rages on— and for some, it always will.

LITERARY GHOSTS

The ghost story is one of the most popular types of fiction, and tales featuring specters and spooks date back eons. Hundreds of supernatural thrillers have been penned through the years, some of them by literature's most influential writers, including Edgar Allan Poe, Ambrose Bierce, and Charles Dickens. Read on for a more detailed look at how the ghost story has shaped literature.

HAUNTING HOMER

In Homer's epic poem *The Odyssey*, the hero Odysseus encounters three ghosts after digging a special pit to honor Greek gods Hades and Persephone. The specters include his mother, who died while he was away, and the spirit of a ship-mate whose body had been left unburied on Circe's Island. The third ghost is that of blind prophet Tiresias, who warns Odysseus about what lies ahead during his journey home.

SHOCKING SHAKESPEARE

Spirits are also common characters in the works of William Shakespeare. In fact, two of Shakespeare's most popular plays—*Hamlet* and *Macbeth*—feature ghosts in pivotal roles.

The ghost of Hamlet's father appears several times in *Hamlet* to provide his son with information about his demise. *Macbeth* is also full of supernatural characters, including the spirit of Banquo and several apparitions conjured up by the witches who give Macbeth a sneak peek at his future.

The Haunted Mind of Edgar Allan Poe

Although he died in 1849, Edgar Allan Poe remains one of the world's best-known writers of horror fiction. His stories have inspired numerous movies, television shows, and literary works.

Poe was a master of the Gothic style of horror, in which characters slowly descend into madness that often leads to horrific consequences. His short stories and poems are filled with individuals who are driven to the brink of insanity.

"The Fall of the House of Usher" is a prime example of this style. First published in 1839, it's the tale of a man named Roderick Usher, who suffers from an unknown illness. His sister Madeline is also ill and often falls into deathlike trances.

After Madeline dies, her body is put in the family tomb for two weeks before her burial. During that time, Roderick experiences unexplained phenomena, including horrific sounds that echo throughout the house. Eventually, Roderick becomes convinced that his sister—whom he admits he entombed while she was still alive—is responsible. When Madeline arrives at Roderick's bedroom door, the reader must decide if she's really dead or if she's still alive.

Edgar Allan Poe never failed to deliver haunting descriptions of the grotesque and macabre. As a result, his stories and poems send shivers down the spines of even the most skeptical readers.

DICKENSIAN SPOOKS

Charles Dickens is best known for his non-supernatural works of fiction, including *Oliver Twist, David Copperfield, Great Expectations,* and *A Tale of Two Cities.* But, like Shakespeare, he wasn't afraid of ghosts. In fact, Dickens was so fascinated by the paranormal that, over the course of his career, he wrote 20 short stories starring ghosts, including "The Signalman," which is considered a classic of the genre.

Of course, short stories weren't Dickens's only contributions to horror fiction. *A Christmas Carol* features four famous apparitions: Ebenezer Scrooge's deceased business partner Jacob Marley and the ghosts of Christmas Past, Present, and Future, all of whom conspire to make the heartless, penny-pinching Scrooge a better person.

HENRY JAMES'S HAUNTED HEROINE

In 1898, Henry James—another Victorian-era literary genius—penned one of his best-known works, *The Turn of the Screw.* This story concerns a nanny who's in charge of caring for two children at their isolated country home. Shortly after starting her job, the nanny sees a strange man glaring at her, first from a tower attached to the house and then through a window. A maid identifies the specter as that of Peter Quint, a deceased servant.

Convinced that the spirit of Quint and the ghost of the nanny who came before her (which she also sees) are after them, the nanny becomes increasingly protective of the children in her care. The specters make their presence known throughout the story, which ends in tragedy. The tale leaves the reader wondering whether the apparitions were real or merely a figment of the nanny's imagination.

GHOSTS IN THE COMICS

In the 1950s, ghost stories became very popular in American comic books. With sales of titles starring superheroes on the decline, publishers turned to horror and science fiction to try to retain readers. The results were remarkable. Titles such as *Tales from the Crypt, Weird Mysteries*, and *Menace* filled the racks, and kids couldn't get enough. In fact, during the heyday of the horror-inspired comic book (1950–1955), between 50 and 100 terrifying tales were released monthly, many of them variations on the traditional ghost story. In the early 1970s, the comic-book industry saw an increase in the popularity of supernatural stories after the easing of the Comics Code, which earlier had banned words such as *horror* and *terror* from comic-book covers.

HILL HOUSE MEETS HELL HOUSE

In 1959, Shirley Jackson published a landmark ghost story titled *The Haunting of Hill House.* It's about a group of para-normal investigators, led by Dr. John Montague, who stay in Hill House in an attempt to determine what's causing the supernatural occurrences reported there. It quickly becomes apparent that the house contains an otherworldly entity and that it has a thing for one member of the investigative team—a troubled young woman named Eleanor.

The Haunting of Hill House has twice been adapted for the silver screen—once in 1963 and again in 1999. Both versions were titled *The Haunting.* The remarkable book inspired another classic of the genre: *Hell House* (1971), which was penned by acclaimed fantasy writer Richard Matheson.

Hell House also concerns a group of paranormal researchers. However, in this tale, they are hired by a terminally ill millionaire to investigate whether there is life after death. The researchers do this by moving into the spooky Belasco House, which, according to the story, is considered to be the most haunted house in the world. The mansion is home to a very evil spirit, but unlike the ghost in *The Haunting of Hill House,* which mostly played mind games with its victims, the specter haunting Belasco House is physically violent toward its unwanted guests.

THREE MEN AND AN ANGRY GHOST

Twenty years after Shirley Jackson published *The Haunting of Hill House,* novelist Peter Straub upped the ante with his best seller *Ghost Story.* It's about three elderly men who share a horrible secret from their youth: They accidentally killed a young woman whom they all knew. Many decades later, the spirit of the woman returns to get revenge on her killers and those who helped cover up her death.

Ghosts have long been—and remain—a popular topic in literature for one main reason: Readers love to be scared. What's the most terrifying tale ever written? That's a matter of opinion. But in the eyes of most, the best ghost stories are the ones that turn readers' knuckles as white as the things that go bump in the night.

THE WORRIED HUSBAND

"You never pay any attention to me!" is a common grievance in marriages when a person feels neglected by his or her partner. But what about the opposite situation—when a person's concern for his or her spouse extends beyond the grave?

In the late 1940s, Elaine and her husband lived in an apartment in Oskaloosa, Iowa. They shared the floor with a single woman named Patricia, whose husband had died in an industrial accident. The devastated young woman had moved there to try to make a fresh start.

One evening while her husband was working, Elaine decided to take a bath. Just as she was about to turn on the bathroom light, she smelled pipe smoke and then saw a young man with black hair and a horseshoe-shaped scar on his cheek. He was holding a pipe.

Elaine soon realized that the man was not really looking *at* her, he was looking *through* her. That's when she realized that he was a ghost. Elaine watched as he moved through her apartment and glided down the hall toward Patricia's place. When he got to Patricia's door, he vanished.

Uncertain of what she was doing, Elaine turned the doorknob to Patricia's apartment. It was unlocked, so Elaine went inside. There, she found Patricia lying on her bed, barely alive. She had tried to kill herself, and her lifeblood was quickly draining away. Elaine bandaged Patricia as best she could and called her husband. He raced home with a doctor, who treated Patricia's injuries.

The next day, Patricia thanked Elaine for saving her life. She said that she had been deeply saddened by her husband's death and had been drinking as a result. Overcome by grief, the idea of joining her husband seemed appealing to her. If it had not been for Elaine, her plan would have succeeded.

Elaine said nothing about why she had entered Patricia's apartment in the first place. But when Patricia showed Elaine a picture of her dead husband, everything suddenly made sense. The man in the photo was the same man Elaine had seen in her apartment.

GHOST DOGS

Many people are afraid of dogs. But the following is a list of places where, if you're not careful, you might find yourself staring down a ghostly canine that has stuck around after passing away.

WOODLAND CEMETERY

There's something to be said for the unconditional love that's shared between a boy and his dog. A prime example of this is the story of five-year-old Johnny Morehouse and his scruffy pooch. In the mid-1800s, Johnny could often be seen playing by the Miami & Erie Canal near Dayton, Ohio, with his faithful dog beside him. One morning in 1860, Johnny slipped and fell into the canal's icy water. The dog jumped into the water and tried to save Johnny, but it was too late for the little boy.

Legend has it that after Johnny was laid to rest at Woodland Cemetery in Dayton, his faithful dog refused to leave the grave site. After the dog died in 1861, a monument was erected near Johnny's grave. It shows the boy sleeping while his dog stands over him. Many believe that, even in death, Johnny's dog is still watching over him. Some say the statue often comes to life and that if you place your hand under the dog's nostrils, you can feel it breathing. Others have reported seeing the ghosts of Johnny and his dog running and playing together throughout the cemetery.

PEDDLER'S ROCK

If you ever find yourself in the historic town of Port Tobacco, Maryland, ask the locals to show you the way to Peddler's Rock, where you just might catch a glimpse of a spectral dog—a blue mastiff. A long-standing legend states that a man and his dog were brutally murdered at Peddler's Rock in the 18th century. The culprits were never caught.

It is said that the ghost of the blue mastiff paces back and forth across the top of Peddler's Rock. Occasionally, its loud, bone-chilling howls can be heard piercing the night air.

SUNNYBANK

Albert Payson Terhune was an author who wrote books about dogs, but his devotion to canines went much deeper than that. In 1912, Albert moved to Sunnybank—his family's summer home in New Jersey—and began breeding rough collies. Eventually, Albert became so successful at breeding that he opened Sunnybank Kennels.

Rex was different from the other dogs at the kennel. He wasn't a purebred, but rather a collie/bull terrier mix. Also, Rex had a large, unique scar on his head. Rex loved Albert, and the feeling was mutual. It was often said that if you wanted to know where Albert was, all you had to do was find Rex and Albert wouldn't be far away. That was true even after Rex's death. Shortly after the dog's passing, friends reported seeing his ghost following Albert around the property and even lying at his feet. Those who were unaware that Rex had died even thought the apparition was the real dog. But Albert himself never claimed to see Rex's ghost.

After Albert passed away in 1942, the kennels and the surrounding property fell into disrepair and were eventually sold. Much of the original estate is now a public park. As visitors wander the grounds, they may come across the graves of many of Albert's dogs. Rex's grave isn't marked, but many locals claim to see his ghost wandering through the park.

BORLEY RECTORY

Often called the "Most Haunted House in England," the Borley Rectory was built in the 1860s. It quickly gained a reputation for being home to all sorts of spooks. In the late 1930s, famous ghost hunter Harry Price conducted an investigation there that lasted many months. During that time, Price and his team encountered ghostly nuns, a headless phantom, flying bricks, and a ghost dog. On more than one occasion, Price and his team heard the eerie sound of a hound howling from somewhere inside the building, but no dog was ever found. Several investigators also described seeing a large spectral canine walking slowly across the rectory grounds.

BONAVENTURE CEMETERY

Bonaventure Cemetery is the largest city cemetery in Savannah, Georgia. But the graveyard's real claim to fame is that it was featured in the 1997 movie *Midnight in the Garden of Good and Evil.* It's also a place where ghost dogs are said to prowl.

For many years, a pack of phantom dogs has been known to chase people out of the cemetery, especially if they're trespassing late at night. If the idea of being pursued by a pack of spectral canines isn't spooky enough, consider that no one has ever actually seen the dogs—not even those who have been chased by them. Only their barking and snarling is heard as they draw near. If you'd rather not risk being run down by the ghostly dogs, just roll down your windows as you drive by and listen closely—you just might hear the baying of the hounds.

THE DEADLY DOLL

Many people have suffered bizarre and unusual deaths. But Magda Hamilton's death may be one of the strangest.

In the mid-1800s, Estelle Ridley was a dwarf (or little person) who spent her youth working for the circus. But when she was in her late thirties or early forties, Estelle turned to a life of crime. She used her small size to pose as a young girl in order to smuggle jewels in a doll that she carried. An older woman named Magda Hamilton pretended to be Estelle's nanny. They traveled by ship from Europe to the United

States, where they would sell the jewelry they'd stolen. The innocent-looking Estelle was easily able to hide the jewels in the belly of her doll.

Estelle and Magda made a fortune selling the stolen jewels. But when both women fell for the same man—Dartway Crawley—Magda turned Estelle over to the police. Sentenced to life in prison, Estelle vowed revenge.

Magda married Dartway and moved into the Crawley Mansion on Staten Island in New York. But after only a few months of marriage, Dartway left Magda to mine for gold in California.

In 1870, Estelle killed herself in prison, and a short time later, Magda was found dead in her home. Legend has it that Estelle's ghost suffocated Magda by cramming her doll's head into Magda's mouth. While that seems like a stretch, visitors have reported seeing Estelle's pint-size spirit on the property of the Crawley Mansion ever since.

WHO YA GONNA CALL?

Your house is oozing with ectoplasm. Strange moaning and wailing sounds keep you up at night. Objects move on their own. If you're a fan of old movies, you'll dial up the Ghostbusters—except that these spirit chasers are the real deal.

THE GHOST WHISPERER

Bonnie Vent, the founder of the San Diego Paranormal Research Project, is actually more of a ghost whisperer than a ghost hunter. In fact, she prefers the term "spirit advocate." According to a 2008 article in *The New York Times,* she can cleanse your home of spooky visitors with a little bit of friendly coaxing.

Bonnie doesn't believe in rituals. Instead, she talks to ghosts to find out why they're hanging around. "Spirit people are people," she says. "You have to get to the root cause." Bonnie's services are not cheap. (She charges $125 an hour.) And sometimes, the ghost decides to stick around anyway, in which case she recommends that you "try to work out a livable situation." Conveniently, Bonnie doubles as a real estate agent and invites potential buyers and sellers of haunted houses to advertise on her website.

THE PARANORMAL INVESTIGATOR

If your definition of a "livable situation" includes only the living, call Fiona Broome, who bills herself as a paranormal investigator. Like Bonnie Vent, Fiona recommends talking to the ghost. If that doesn't work, she resorts to an assortment of traditional remedies, including garlic, sea salt, holy water, and hex signs. She also offers this tip: Place your shoes at the foot of the bed pointed in opposite directions. This will apparently cause the ghost to become so confused that it will seek out a more orderly home.

Smudge Sticks Work, Too

Mary Ann Winkowski, another buster of ghosts, suggests burning bundles of white sage, known as smudge sticks, to banish ghosts from the premises. Smudge sticks are used in many Native American cleansing ceremonies. Mary Ann claims that they have helped her to remove ghosts from homes, offices, schools, and even cars. She served as a consultant for the popular television drama *Ghost Whisperer,* as did her fellow psychic, James Van Praagh.

James describes himself as a "clairsentient" which means that he is able to receive information from spirits through his emotions. Unlike other ghost whisperers, James doesn't try to get rid of ghosts. Instead, he tries to locate spirits for those who want to connect with dead loved ones.

Patty A. Wilson of the Ghost Research Foundation spends more time looking for ghosts than getting rid of them. The author of a series of books on ghost hunting in Pennsylvania, she acknowledges that "ghosts' stories are not neat and clean. They're real stories about real people." And they don't always end with the ghost drifting off into the great beyond.

The Amityville Horror: Haunted House or Horrible Hoax?

It seems that nearly every town has a haunted house— the one place that animals and locals avoid like the plague. But when it comes to haunted houses that can give you nightmares for weeks, nothing can hold a ghostly candle to one foreboding Dutch Colonial in Amityville, New York, which once glared down at passersby with windows that seemed to resemble demonic eyes.

Brutal Beginnings

Most hauntings begin with tragic circumstances, and the house at 112 Ocean Avenue is no exception. In the early morning hours of November 13, 1974, someone fatally shot six of the seven members of the DeFeo family—parents Ronald Sr. and Louise and four of their children: Mark, John, Allison, and Dawn. The only family member to escape the massacre was 23-year-old Ronnie "Butch" DeFeo, who was arrested and charged with all six murders. He eventually confessed and was sentenced to 25 years to life in prison. During the trial, rumors suggested that demonic voices had directed Butch to commit the murders, although prosecutors claimed that he was merely trying to collect the family's $200,000 life insurance policy.

The DeFeo house stood unoccupied until December 1975, when new owners moved in.

The Horror Begins

George and Kathy Lutz knew that they had found a bargain when their realtor showed them the house at 112 Ocean Avenue. It had six bedrooms, a pool, and even a boathouse—all for the unbelievable price of $80,000. Of course, an entire family *had* been murdered there, and some of their belongings were still inside, but the Lutzes decided that it was too good a deal to pass up. So George and Kathy moved in with their three young children: Daniel, Christopher, and Missy. Soon after, the family's nightmare began. It quickly became obvious to them that demonic forces were at work inside the house. Here are some of the paranormal events that allegedly took place there:

- George had trouble sleeping and continually woke up at exactly 3:15 A.M., which was believed to be the time that the DeFeo murders took place.

- Missy began talking to an imaginary friend named Jodie, who sometimes appeared as a pig. Standing outside the house one night, George looked up and saw a pig with glowing red eyes staring back at him from Missy's room. (Pigs are often associated with demons.) Later, George found cloven hoofprints in the snow outside the house.

- Even though the family moved in during the middle of winter, certain rooms in the house—especially the sewing room—were constantly infested with flies.

- A small room painted blood-red—which was dubbed "the Red Room"—was found hidden behind shelving in the basement. The Lutzes felt that an evil force inhabited the room. Even the family dog refused to go near it.

- While trying to bless the house, a priest became violently ill and heard an inhuman voice tell him to "Get out!" When George and Kathy attempted to bless the house themselves, they heard voices screaming, "Will you stop?"

- Green slime oozed out of the toilets and walls.

- George unintentionally began to take on the mannerisms of Butch DeFeo. He even grew a beard, which caused him to look like the murderer. Apparently the likeness was so strong that when George walked into a bar that Butch used to frequent, customers thought he *was* Butch.

Freaked out by the unseen forces at work in the home, the Lutz family left the house in the middle of the night on January 14, 1976. The following day, George sent movers to collect their belongings. The Lutzes never again set foot inside the house at 112 Ocean Avenue.

Searching for Evil

In an attempt to understand exactly what had happened to his family inside the house, George hired paranormal experts Ed and Lorraine Warren, who arrived in Amityville with a local news crew on March 6, 1976. Lorraine said that she sensed a very strong evil presence in the house. Several years later, the Warrens released photos from the investigation that seem to show a ghostly boy with glowing eyes standing near one of the staircases.

In September 1977, author Jay Anson released a book titled *The Amityville Horror: A True Story.* It chronicles the Lutz family's harrowing ordeal and was compiled from more than 40 hours of tape-recorded interviews with George and Kathy. It became a best seller almost immediately. But it didn't take long before people started taking a closer look into what really happened at 112 Ocean Avenue.

The Controversy Begins

When people started to scrutinize the specifics in Anson's book, the story began to fall apart. For example, a check of weather conditions showed that there was no snow on the ground when George claimed to have found the strange cloven footprints outside the house. Likewise, windows and doors that ghostly forces had supposedly broken were found to be intact. Reporters who interviewed neighbors along Ocean Avenue found that not a single person could remember seeing or hearing anything strange going on at the house. And despite the book mentioning numerous visits by the local police to investigate strange noises at the house, the Amityville Police Department publicly stated that during the time the Lutzes lived there, they never once visited the home or received a single phone call from the family.

The Lawsuits

In May 1977, the Lutzes filed a series of lawsuits against several publications and individuals who had either investigated 112 Ocean Avenue or had written about the reported hauntings there. They said that those accused had invaded their privacy and caused their family mental distress. There was one other name in the lawsuits that raised a few eyebrows: William Weber, Butch DeFeo's defense attorney.

Even more surprising was that Weber filed a countersuit for $2 million for breach of contract. He contended that he had met with the Lutzes and, together, they made up the story of the house being haunted. He sued them when he found out that they had taken their story to Jay Anson and essentially cut him out of the book deal. In September 1979, a U.S. District Court judge dismissed all of the Lutzes' claims and made some notable remarks in his ruling, including his belief that the book was basically a work of fiction. Weber's countersuit was later settled out of court.

What Really Happened?

Even though it's been decades since the Lutzes occupied the house at 112 Ocean Avenue, many questions still remain. A series of books and films bearing the name *The Amityville Horror* continue to blur the lines between what really happened in the home and what was made up. In 2005, a remake of the original *Amityville Horror* movie added many new elements to the story that are questionable.

Kathy Lutz died in August 2004, and George passed away in May 2006. Both went to their graves claiming that what they said happened to them at 112 Ocean Avenue was not a hoax.

The house itself still stands. One would think that a building as infamous as the "Amityville Horror" house would be easy to find. Not so. In order to stop the onslaught of trespassing curiosity seekers, its address has been changed, so 112 Ocean Avenue technically no longer exists. Also, the distinctive quarter-moon windows have been removed and replaced with ordinary square ones.

Since the Lutz family moved out, the property has changed hands several times, and none of the subsequent owners have reported any paranormal activity. Some have been frightened from time to time, but that's usually due to trespassers peering into the windows of this allegedly haunted house.

SHARE A TOAST WITH A GHOST

Visitors to the Golden Fleece pub and inn in York, England, can spend a few minutes or a full night with numerous ghosts at the town's most haunted site. Built in the 16th century, the Golden Fleece is a well-kept but ancient building surrounded by a mysterious atmosphere.

Enjoy Some Spirits

Upon entering the Golden Fleece, visitors sense spirits from the pub's past. Even when the front room is nearly empty, many visitors glance around nervously, expecting to see other guests standing in a dark corner. Unexplained shadows move and then vanish, and the sound of phantom glasses clinking can be heard. It's truly an eerie place.

Many guests will witness the Golden Fleece's spooks if they go looking for them. Ghosts have been reported in every part of the pub and also in the yard behind it. Most people see the spirits as flickering figures, off to one side. Others see full apparitions, such as the colorful ghost of Lady Alice Peckett.

Lady Peckett Kept Her Head, But Thomas Percy Didn't

Lady Alice Peckett haunts both the Golden Fleece and Lady Peckett's Yard, which is located directly behind the pub. Her husband, John, who owned the building, was the Lord Mayor of the city of York in 1701. He left the pub when he died, but his wife decided to stay. No one is certain why she lingers, but some claim that she was too spirited and fun-loving for her more serious politician husband. Perhaps she doesn't want to miss out on anything at the Golden Fleece.

Lady Alice generally manifests as an older woman wearing sweet perfume, but don't let her sunny personality fool you. She's a mischievous ghost who likes to surprise people by walking through walls.

Another ghost to keep an eye out for is Thomas Percy. He's a relatively harmless spirit who floats around near the entrance to the Golden Fleece in search of his missing head.

During the reign of Queen Elizabeth I, when Catholics were burned at the stake, Thomas held strong to his Catholic beliefs. Even so, he was a favorite of Elizabeth for many years. But in 1569, he led a rebellion against the queen and planned to replace her with her Catholic cousin, Mary, Queen of Scots. After the rebellion failed, Thomas was beheaded not far from the Golden Fleece. Although his body was buried, his head was left on public display as a warning to others. After some time, the head was simply thrown away.

A FINE "COLD SPOT" IN THE PUB

If the weather is warm, find a seat at the booth in the back corner of the pub. The spirits like to keep that corner cool and breezy. During a June 2007 visit, a group of American tourists complimented the staff on how well the booth was cooled. They were startled to learn that there is no air conditioning in the pub.

The chilling effect may be thanks to "One Eyed Jack," a 17th-century ghost dressed in a red coat, a wig, and crisply pressed trousers. He creates a refreshing breeze as he paces up and down the room carrying a pistol and waiting to be served.

A Full Night of Good Spirits

If you have the courage, you can spend the night at the inn above the pub. Look for the gruesome, blue-tinted face of a World War II airman who fell to his death from a window. Or listen for the confused whimpering of a little boy who appears in Victorian clothing. In the late 1800s, he was crushed to death when a cart backed up to the pub door to make a delivery. He's often seen around the front room of the pub and has even been known to pick pockets.

If you encounter a ghost wearing a noose, it has escaped from the pub's basement, where corpses were sometimes stored. Many of the bodies were never claimed, and they may be buried there. Perhaps they're wandering the Golden Fleece hoping that someone will give them a proper burial.

Overnight guests often hear music and loud laughter coming from the pub. When they investigate the noise, they discover that the pub is closed, the lights are off, and the downstairs rooms are empty…unless you count the ghosts, of course.

Just remember that if you see a Roman soldier who seems to be walking on his knees, nothing terrible happened to his legs. He's simply from a time when the streets of York were several feet lower than they are now. That's the level where his ghostly feet are.

Ghosts of the *Titanic* Exhibit—
Just the Tip of the Haunted Iceberg

On April 14, 1912, the supposedly unsinkable RMS Titanic struck an iceberg in the North Atlantic. By the end of the next day, nearly 1,500 souls lay in a cold, watery grave. Nestled deep in frigid waters, the wreckage sat undisturbed until it was discovered on the ocean floor in 1985.

Recovering the Wreckage

Since the wreckage of the *Titanic* was located, divers have recovered about 5,900 items from the site. Many of these objects are included in *Titanic: The Artifact Exhibition,* which has traveled the world since the early 1990s—and a few ghosts have gone along for the ride.

Haunting Atlanta

When the exhibit traveled to Atlanta, a volunteer said she sensed that lost souls were embedded in the artifacts. She also felt a hand moving over her head and touching her hair. And a four-year-old boy repeatedly asked his mother and grandmother about a lady that he saw in a display case, which—to the adults—held only a dress and a sofa. Another visitor saw a man in a black-and-white suit who seemed out of place amongst the other, more casually dressed people. Later, when she felt as if she was being watched, the visitor turned around to see the man in the suit staring at her.

In 2008, a paranormal investigation team saw shadowy figures and picked up the voices of spirits on audio recordings. They concluded that at least three ghosts are attached to the exhibit—those of an older gentleman, an elderly woman, and a young crew member.

Jason Hawes and Grant Wilson and their team from The Atlantic Paranormal Society (TAPS) also investigated the exhibit. Their findings, which aired on a 2009 episode of *Ghost Hunters*, were similar to those of other researchers. In the Iceberg Exhibit (which contains a replica of an iceberg to give visitors a sense of what one feels like), Jason and Grant detected a moving cold spot that seemed to be four to five feet tall and one to two feet wide. Jason also felt something tug on his shirt. While in the Artifacts Exhibit, both investigators saw a shadowy figure walk into another room, and Jason felt an unseen hand touch his shoulder. Before they left the room, Jason asked the spirit to knock on the wall if it wanted them to leave. They heard nothing, but their audio recorder picked up an EVP that sounded like a man whispering, "No, please wait," or perhaps even, "Don't leave me." In the end, they concluded that ghosts were definitely present and are likely attached to the *Titanic* exhibit.

ROCKING NEW YORK CITY

When the exhibit moved to New York City, motion-activated security cameras clicked on every night at 3 A.M., even though no living being was present. And one visitor said that as she and her cousin walked through a hallway, they felt a rocking sensation, as if they were really on a ship. They asked if this was some sort of special effect. It wasn't, but they were told that many other people had asked the same question.

CHILLING ST. PAUL

When the artifacts visited St. Paul, Minnesota, one visitor left the Iceberg Exhibit because she suddenly felt dizzy. Then, she felt a hand touching her shoulder, even though no one else was around. Her shoulder felt cold and then hot, as if she had frostbite. A few minutes later, a red mark appeared on her shoulder. Another person reported similar sensations when leaving the Iceberg Exhibit, including dizziness, taps on the shoulder, and the queasy sensation of being rocked.

GHOSTS IN BRANSON

Even a permanent *Titanic* museum in Branson, Missouri, is said to be teeming with ghosts. This re-creation of the legendary ship displays approximately 400 artifacts from the *Titanic* and is thought to be home to at least one ghost-child. Members of the cleaning staff have found child-size fingerprints on the glass separating the Promenade Deck and the Bridge. Many children visit the museum, so this is not unusual. But the prints reappear after the glass is cleaned while the museum is closed. One staff member even photo-graphed a wet footprint in the shape of a child's bare foot.

Ghosts have also been spotted in other parts of the ship: A man in formal wear has been seen at the top of the Grande Staircase and a lady in a gown glides around the First Class Dining Salon and emerges from the area carrying her belongings. And even though the museum has a no smoking policy, both staffers and visitors have smelled cigar smoke around the Grande Staircase on numerous occasions.

To determine once and for all if ghosts from the *Titanic* haunt the museum, the owners invited two different teams of paranormal investigators to conduct research overnight. Both teams found high psychic-energy levels that became higher when staff members asked the spirits questions. As museum staffers communicated with two passengers who died on the ship, one of them became weak and nauseous.

FINAL ATTACHMENTS

When the exhibit visited Athens, Greece, employees heard English-speaking voices in the museum after hours. And in Monterrey, Mexico, several people commented on a man who they thought was an actor dressed in a black suit that would have been fashionable in 1912. However, the exhibit did not employ any reenactors.

It makes sense that the *Titanic*'s victims would follow the items that they knew in life and rested with in death for many decades. The artifacts will continue to travel the world as long as there is interest in them, but hopefully, the spirits will eventually separate themselves from their earthly belongings and finally rest in peace.

AMERICA FROM GHOST-TO-GHOST

People have been chasing ghosts for centuries, but these days, there is no shortage of books, movies, television shows, and paranormal research groups that offer insight into the unknown.

No matter where you are in the United States, chances are good that you'll find a number of legends attached to your hometown. The details of the stories may differ, but you can find something spooky anywhere in the nation.

THE EAST COAST
Take New York City, for example. The city is world-renowned for Broadway and the theater. Not as well known are the stories of ghosts that call the Big Apple home.

At the Belasco Theatre on 44th Street, there's at least one person who's no longer living that still shows up for every curtain call. That's former owner David Belasco, who built the playhouse in 1907. David was so passionate about the theater that he has continued to attend every opening night since his death in 1931. Sometimes, his spirit is accompanied by that of a woman known simply as the "Blue Lady."

The New Amsterdam Theater on West 42nd Street is said to be haunted by the ghost of a chorus singer. Olive Thomas apparently committed suicide in the place where she was happiest in life. Dressed in her green beaded stage gown and headpiece, she wanders through the building after the final curtain call carrying a blue bottle of pills.

The internationally known Palace Theatre on Broadway is said to be home to more than a hundred spirits, including that of singer/actress Judy Garland, who apparently still hovers by the stage door—perhaps waiting for her fans. However, there's one ghost that no one wants to encounter: the acrobat who broke his neck onstage. According to legend, anyone who sees him will die soon afterward.

The West Coast

Travel west to California and you'll find a haunted site that annually attracts more than a million visitors. Alcatraz— the forbidding facility that sits on a barren, rocky island in San Francisco Bay—was America's most infamous prison between 1934 and 1963. During that time, it served as the home of notorious criminals, such as Al Capone and George "Machine Gun" Kelly. Perhaps a few of them haven't left.

Visitors have felt cold spots as they enter the cell house through double steel doors. In C Block, a metal door that had been welded shut leads to an area that is reportedly haunted by three convicts who were killed during a 1946 escape attempt. Over the years, guards reported eerie sounds, including crying and moaning from empty cells. And phantom figures have been seen walking the corridors late at night.

One of the most psychically charged areas at Alcatraz is "the Hole," the place where prisoners who broke the rules were punished. Cell 14D, one of the four-foot-by-eight-foot underground cells, is noticeably colder than the others. A supernatural presence is believed to have existed there since the 1940s—ever since the night an inmate screamed that a ghost with glowing eyes was locked inside the cell with him. The guards had always joked about a phantom haunting that area, but no one was laughing when they opened the cell the next morning to find the inmate dead with hand marks on his neck.

Although the cause of death was listed as strangulation, no earthly or unearthly source was ever discovered that could have caused his death. What happened the next day was equally perplexing. During roll call, the guards noticed that one extra convict kept appearing in line—the man who had died the night before. As the guards and inmates watched, he vanished before their eyes. His ghost is reportedly still imprisoned in the Hole.

Down South

Many believe that New Orleans, Louisiana, is the capital of America's supernatural world. Even skeptics change their minds after a visit to the city's French Quarter.

What lurks there, aside from the beautiful, centuries-old buildings, the music, and the nightlife? Take a "ghost tour" of this part of the city and find out. First settled by the French in the early 18th century, the Quarter has been home to a host of memorable characters, some who apparently refuse to leave—even after death. Voodoo priestess Marie Laveau, who captivated the city in the early 19th century, is buried in St. Louis Cemetery No. 2, and her spirit is said to linger close by. Many people believe that she will answer the prayers of anyone who leaves an offering at her grave.

At the heart of the French Quarter stands a mansion that once belonged to the LaLauries, a popular couple who lived there in the 1830s. When a fire broke out during a party in 1834, guests were shocked to discover terrified slaves chained up in a secret room. It seems that the LaLauries also enjoyed torturing and conducting medical experiments on their servants, some of whom had been held captive for years. Infuriated local residents were ready to lynch the couple when they learned of the abuse, but the LaLauries managed to get away. The ghosts of their victims are said to still roam the house, reenacting the most horrific moments of their lives.

If the thought of coming face-to-face with a few ghosts isn't too alarming, you might want to visit some of these locations and others like them. Just remember—you can shut off the television or put down a scary book, but it's not as easy to walk away from the real thing.

PHANTOM PATIENTS HAUNT THESE HOSPITALS

Considering how many deaths occur at hospitals, it's not surprising that they're home to many restless spirits. Here are some of the most haunted hospitals in the United States.

NATIONWIDE CHILDREN'S HOSPITAL (COLUMBUS, OHIO)

It is rumored that Nationwide Children's Hospital was built on top of an old cemetery, so it's no surprise that some rooms are said to be haunted. Many nurses even avoid certain hallways after dark. People have also reported seeing moving shadows and the figure of a ghostly woman gliding through Livingston Park next door. Many children—who are often more sensitive to seeing spirits than adults—have told of watching this "pink lady" from their hospital windows. This misty spirit effortlessly floats through the trees and over the tombstones. The park sits on a piece of land that was part of an old Confederate cemetery, so perhaps she's looking for a husband or relative who died during the Civil War.

Heather Hill Hospital (Chardon, Ohio)

When patients in the C wing at Heather Hill Hospital tell the nursing staff about a young boy who runs wild in the halls and knocks on the walls of their rooms, they don't get much help with the problem. After all, they can hardly discipline a boy they can't see. Most likely, the mischievous boy is the ghost of a former patient. He is dressed in knickers circa the early 1900s, but no one seems to know who he was in life.

Old Riverside Hospital (Trenton, Michigan)

In 1944, the Church family home in Trenton was converted into a hospital. While the Churches lived there, their daughter had a horse, which she loved dearly. But when she fell off the horse and broke her arm, her father blamed the animal, so he shot it. After that, the girl was so sad that she kept to her room, mournfully singing and gazing out the window.

Patients who have stayed in her former bedroom have heard phantom footsteps and singing. The building was closed in 2002 and is now vacant, but passersby who glance up at the girl's former window have seen a young, curly-haired girl looking back at them. She likes to move the blinds up and down, and if you listen closely, you might hear her singing.

North Carolina Orthopedic Hospital (Gastonia, North Carolina)

The North Carolina Orthopedic Hospital closed in 1979, and its supernatural secrets remained buried until after it was renovated and repurposed. When the Gaston County

Welfare Office moved there in 1982, unusual things started happening. Apparently, the resident ghosts don't know that the building is no longer a hospital. Phantom nurses have been seen moving between the rooms on the second floor. And the Gastonia police have received numerous calls claiming that people are inside the building late at night. But, of course, when officers go to investigate, they find the place empty... or at least that's how it appears.

YORKTOWN MEMORIAL HOSPITAL (YORKTOWN, TEXAS)

Yorktown Memorial Hospital was built in 1950 but has stood empty since it closed in the late 1980s. Caretaker Mike Hanson has reported ghostly experiences there, especially near the nurses' station. He says that the place appears empty while he's making his rounds... until he turns the lights off. In the dark, he's seen shadow figures, phantom patients, and spectral visitors mingling in the hallways. A stairway behind a glass door may also be home to a spirit or two. People have heard unexplained tapping on the glass even though no one is behind the door. In 2009, the Central Texas Ghost Hunters paid a visit to Yorktown Memorial Hospital. They didn't see any apparitions during their visit, but they did capture the sound of organ music coming from the empty chapel. Do these ghosts linger on, still hoping for cures to their ailments?

THE CURSE OF GRIFFITH PARK

Griffith Park in Los Angeles, California, is one of the largest urban parks in America. Many who visit it snap photos of the Hollywood sign, take in the view of the city, gaze at the heavens at the Griffith Observatory, and marvel at the animals at the Los Angeles Zoo. But others leave their visits to the park with bone-chilling tales of ghostly encounters.

WHERE THERE'S A WILL...

The dark history of Griffith Park began in 1863, when it was called Rancho Los Feliz. That was the year when the ranch's owner, Don Antonio Feliz, passed from this world. Many expected that his niece Doña Petranilla would inherit his fortune. But what Petranilla didn't know is that local lawyer Don Antonio Coronel had helped her uncle rewrite his will. After Feliz died, most of his wealth and property went to Coronel. Petranilla was outraged, and she laid a curse upon the land that is still felt to this day.

A CURSE FIT FOR A COLONEL

Following Petranilla's curse, the Coronels and other subsequent owners were all plagued with misfortune and disease until Colonel Griffith J. Griffith purchased the property in 1882. When Griffith acquired the land, his first order of business was to build housing developments, but that venture soon failed. Griffith also allowed a small ostrich farm to open on the property, and it was quite successful. But in 1884, storms plagued the area and the ostriches stampeded every night. Ranch hands claimed that the cause of the ruckus was a phantom rider who appeared in the rain. Some said it was the ghost of Don Feliz, but others believed it was Doña Petranilla, back from the dead to fulfill the curse she had imposed on the land. Regardless of who it was, Griffith refused to visit the property except during the day. Finally, in 1896, he decided to rid himself of the ghost once and for all, so he donated 3,015 acres of his land to the city of Los Angeles.

But that didn't stop the spirit from making appearances from time to time. In 1898, when the city's wealthy and influential residents gathered for a fiesta at Griffith Park, an ethereal horseback rider chased them away. Over the years, many visitors to the park have reported seeing this specter sitting atop a horse and roaming the park's trails or riding through the park at night.

Unfortunately, Griffith's mind deteriorated after that. In 1903, he tried to kill his wife because he thought that she was conspiring against him with the Pope. He spent nearly two years in prison for the crime. When he died in 1919, Colonel Griffith left his remaining fortune to the city of Los Angeles. But if he relieved himself of the cursed property in an attempt to please its restless spirits, the maneuver seems to have failed.

To Live and Die in Hollywood

In the 1930s, Griffith Park claimed another victim. Like so many others, Peg Entwistle had come to Hollywood to realize her dream of seeing her face on the silver screen. But after receiving poor reviews for her performance in her first film, Peg concluded that her movie career was a failure. And so, on the night of September 16, 1932, she climbed to the top of the Hollywood sign's "H" and leaped to her death. A suicide note was found in her purse, and within days, she had achieved the fame that had escaped her in life.

Over the years, several hikers and park rangers have reported seeing a woman dressed in 1930s-era attire near the sign. And from time to time, a spectral blonde woman has been known to set off motion sensors located near the sign. When the rangers investigate, they notice the scent of gardenias.

The City of Angels' Lady in White

Park rangers spend more time in Griffith Park than anyone else, and they know that they're not alone. At their headquarters in the old Feliz home, the rangers have reportedly caught glimpses of a ghostly Hispanic woman who is dressed all in white. Most people seem to think that this is the tormented spirit of Doña Petranilla, the woman who originally cursed the land back in 1863. She died soon after placing the curse, and she is one of the property's oldest lost souls. Griffith's ranch hands witnessed the Lady in White cursing the land and all who lived on it, just as she had done in life. Some have reported hearing her wailing near the Los Angeles Zoo and the golf course, but her favorite haunt seems to be her former home. Although the park is closed at night, Petranilla seems to prefer to make nocturnal appearances, and like her uncle and Colonel Griffith, she is sometimes seen on horseback going for a midnight ride.

REVERSING THE CURSE

Those who might avoid one of the nation's most beautiful public parks for fear of its ghosts probably shouldn't. Most of the spirits that haunt the grounds of Griffith Park seem to visit at night after the park is closed. Also, many movies and television shows have been filmed there over the years, all without a single apparition having been captured on film. In the years since the land passed from Colonel Griffith to the city of Los Angeles, no mysterious tragedies have befallen visitors to the park. But if you find yourself on the property at night—perhaps hiking in view of the Hollywood sign or the historic Feliz home—know that there's a good chance you're not alone.

Spooks that Roam the Stacks

While at work, librarians strive to maintain volume levels that can be described as "tomblike." But if those beings that actually reside in tombs want to raise a ruckus, no librarian in the world can stop them.

Amelia Gayle Gorgas Library, University of Alabama (Tuscaloosa, Alabama)

From 1883 to 1907, Amelia Gayle Gorgas served as the first female librarian at the University of Alabama. She is believed to haunt this facility, which was built in 1939 and named in her honor. She makes her presence known by stopping the elevator on the floor that holds the special collections—even when the elevator bank is locked down. When the doors open, the errant elevator is always empty.

Steubenville Public Library (Steubenville, Ohio)

Ellen Summers Wilson served as the first librarian at the Steubenville Public Library when it opened in 1902. Tragically, she died of tuberculosis only two years later at age 31. Almost immediately after her death, people began hearing footsteps and creaking floorboards coming from the library's attic, which was always found to be empty. In subsequent years, air-conditioning equipment was placed in the attic, and it repeatedly and mysteriously turned off on its own. Eventually, the AC unit was moved to another room, and the ventilation problems ceased.

LEE COUNTY LIBRARY (TUPELO, MISSISSIPPI)

The Lee County Library was constructed in 1971 on the site of the former home of Congressman John Mills Allen. Although the house was torn down, some of its original features were used for the library, including the glass panels and doors in the Mississippi Room. Apparently, Allen's spirit remains as well. Whenever staff members find books removed from shelves and spread across the floor, the congressman is deemed responsible. His ghost is also blamed for removing items from the book drop.

DETROIT PUBLIC LIBRARY–SKILLMAN BRANCH (DETROIT, MICHIGAN)

The Skillman Branch of the Detroit Public Library occupies the site of a former jailhouse where prisoners were routinely executed in the early 1800s. These tormented souls make their presence known by moaning and mumbling. They can be so disruptive that the bookshelves sometimes reverberate with the unsettling sounds.

THE CARNEGIE LIBRARY BRANCH OF THE ST. JOSEPH PUBLIC LIBRARY (ST. JOSEPH, MISSOURI)

After hours, the ghostly footsteps of "Rose," who is thought to be a former librarian, can be heard shuffling across the second floor of the Carnegie Library in St. Joseph, Missouri. Although Rose is also blamed for phantom whispers and giggles, she takes her job very seriously and has been known to shush patrons. Rose also likes to put books back on the shelves, but she often puts them in the wrong place.

Raritan Public Library (Raritan, New Jersey)

Built in the early 1700s, General John Frelinghuysen's former house became the Raritan Public Library in the 1970s. When the library is closed, an unseen presence likes to turn on the lights and move the books. In addition, the apparition of an elderly woman is often seen in a window and in the library's garden. In 1999, paranormal investigators verified that several spirits haunt the building.

James D. Hoskins Library (Knoxville, Tennessee)

It can be scary after hours at the James D. Hoskins Library on the campus of the University of Tennessee because that's when the spooks come out. Doors shut on their own, and maintenance workers have heard the footsteps of the spirit of a former graduate student known as the "Evening Primrose." This ghost apparently likes to cook late at night because custodians and other employees have reported the inexplicable scent of cornbread baking.

Out of Body, Out of Mind?

Does having an out-of-body experience (OBE) mean that you're out of your mind? Absolutely not. In fact, studies show that between 5 and 35 percent of the population has had at least one OBE. And many of the people who have had them don't even know it.

So What the Heck Is an OBE Anyway?

Definitions in scientific journals can get pretty technical, but the simple explanation of an out-of-body experience is that it's the feeling that you've left your physical body and can see yourself and the world from outside of your earthly vessel. Some people describe the OBE as a state in which a person's consciousness separates from his or her body, usually for a very short period of time. Sometimes those who have experienced an OBE report hearing or seeing things that they couldn't have seen or heard from within their own body because their body was in a different location from where the action took place.

People seem to find out-of-body experiences fascinating, but we don't really know much about what causes them. What *is* clear is that an OBE can happen to anyone at any time. And although an OBE can occur during a near-death experience (NDE), the two are not one and the same. An OBE occurs when the mind separates from the physical body, but the spirit remains in the physical world. During a near-death experience, the person may or may not experience an OBE. The individual may look down at her body lying in a hospital bed or see herself in a wrecked car, which would be an OBE, but the rest of the NDE involves *leaving* the physical world and traveling to "the Other Side." Most people who experience NDEs report seeing a bright light, traveling through a tunnel, and seeing deceased relatives. Those components are not part of a simple OBE, during which the person remains in this realm.

One survey asked people who'd had OBEs to describe the circumstances surrounding them. More than 85 percent of respondents said that they'd had their OBEs while they were resting, sleeping, or dreaming. Others reported being sick in bed or even medicated. But still other people—especially those moving at fast speeds, like in an airplane or on a motorcycle—have reported feeling as if they were floating above themselves.

Do It Yourself...or Not

While many OBEs simply occur, researchers have confirmed that some people are able to create their own out-of-body experiences by using relaxation techniques. Those who can do this at will report a greater feeling of control, as if they are out of their regular body but remain empowered in the situation. Many even describe a "silver cord" that attaches their physical body to their spiritual form. The silver cord and the feeling of empowerment are much less pronounced among those whose OBEs are spontaneous. Many subjects report a sense of great energy. They see bright colors and hear loud noises. Everything is vivid and vibrant, yet more like being awake (except that the person observes it from above) than in a dream. OBEs seem to be more grounded and feel more "real" than dreams.

Tell Me More

We could analyze OBEs and NDEs all day, but it's more
fun to read about actual experiences rather than the science
behind them. Here are some reports from people who have
actually experienced them.

No Fear of Flying

A woman named Eileen said that she had an out-of-body
experience when she was nine, so she wasn't afraid when she
had another one as an adult. When it happened to her as a
child, she simply rose to the ceiling and hovered above her
body. During her adult experience, Eileen was lying near her
grandson, who was very ill. Suddenly, she felt herself leave
her body through the bottoms of her feet. She reported feeling as though she was flying feet-first for a hundred miles.
After a short time, her ethereal form or her soul—which
seemed as though it was still attached—reentered her physical
body. Initially, reconnecting was uncomfortable, but she
eventually settled back in. When she awoke, her body was
lying calmly with its feet crossed, as though she hadn't a care
in the world.

Scared Back to Reality

Although it happened in 1980, Paul said that he remembers
his OBE like it occurred yesterday. He had gone to bed and
was drifting off to sleep when, suddenly, he awoke to hear a
loud humming noise and felt his entire body vibrating. The

next thing he knew, he was looking down at himself and his wife in the bed. He decided to visit an aunt who lived nearby, but on the way, he encountered a strange man who tried to hand him a small scroll. Something about the man or the paper must have frightened Paul because he quickly returned to the bedroom, where he "slammed" back into his body. He said that it was like nothing he had ever experienced before. He's sure he wasn't dreaming, and he hadn't taken any medication or drugs.

ESCAPING EARTHLY ILLNESS FOR A WHILE

Linda had been ill for some time when she decided to stop fighting her disease. No more doctors. No more medication. She was going to be free.

Soon after her decision, Linda had a near-death experience during which she watched her spirit leave her physical body. She could see her diseased body laying there, but she no longer had a connection to it. Suddenly, she felt no pain and she no longer struggled to breathe. As her weightless spirit lifted, so did her depression. Linda felt a profound sense of calm. When she made a conscious decision to let go of

her lifeless body, she felt a powerful force lift her upward. Linda described the rest of her experience as a peaceful journey to heaven, which ended when she claimed that God told her that she must return to earth. She could not recall her trip back to this world, but she has since recovered from her illness.

A CAMPFIRE STORY

A nine-year-old boy had an out-of-body experience while camping and told his mother about it when he returned home. The boy's parents were divorced, and he was on vacation with his father in early 2004. While the youngster was drifting off to sleep, he felt a huge burst of energy. Suddenly, he found himself back at the campfire, where he could see and hear the adults quite clearly. However, glancing back at the tent, he was surprised to see that his body was still inside—fast asleep.

A SPIRITUAL OBE...

Kevin from Toronto described his out-of-body experience as being something of a religious experience. It occurred one night in 1990, when he was feeling especially tired and went to bed a bit earlier than usual. He thought he fell asleep right away, but the sensation that he experienced was not at all like a dream. He "woke up" and realized that he was about six feet above the bed, where his body was still laying. Kevin said he felt an incredible peace and happiness in the moment. He believes his OBE was a message to him that each person's spiritual journey is just a part of life. He remembers that message each and every day.

...And a Spiritual NDE

When Baptist minister Don Piper was on his way home from an out-of-town conference in the early 2000s, his vehicle was hit head-on by an 18-wheeler. Pronounced dead at the scene, his spirit was immediately transported to the Great Beyond. According to his book *90 Minutes in Heaven,* Piper had an out-of-body experience like nothing he had ever imagined. He had no memory of the crash or of hovering above his body. Instead, he said he went directly to heaven and was reunited with deceased friends and relatives. He knew that he was no longer on earth because he was in a place that was more beautiful than anything he had ever seen. All of his senses were heightened, and he recognized people who were no longer living. After 90 minutes, he was sent back to earth, where he found himself awake and in pain, with heaven nothing more than a memory.

Hot Springs and Cool Spirits at the Banff Springs Hotel

Surrounded by majestic mountains and the healing waters of natural hot springs, the Banff Springs Hotel in Alberta, Canada, attracts many visitors...but not everyone staying at the hotel is among the living.

In the late 1800s, William Van Horne was the general manager of the Canadian Pacific Railway. He decided to take advantage of the railroads' westward expansion by building a 250-room luxury hotel tucked away in the dense forest of the Canadian Rockies. The Banff Springs Hotel was a success, but in 1926, it was partially destroyed by a devastating fire. When it was rebuilt, the hotel took on the look of a Scottish castle. Stone walls and grand towers added a touch of class and mystery that was missing from the first building. This time, the hotel became even more successful. And due to its isolated location, it attracted royalty and celebrities who often referred to it as the "Castle of the Rockies."

THE SECRET ROOM

During the renovation, construction workers were surprised to discover a secret room that did not appear on any maps of the hotel. It resembled a regular guest room, except that it had no windows or doors. This mysterious room is thought to have been an architectural error that was sealed off—and removed from blueprints—to cover up the mistake. Although the room was empty when it was discovered, many people who had experienced unusual phenomena—such as strange noises and apparitions—along a nearby corridor suspected that perhaps something about this odd room could be the cause. Did something sinister happen inside the room? Were spirits using it as a portal to the Other Side?

Regardless of the secret room's purpose, many ghosts call the Banff Springs Hotel home. But that doesn't seem to keep guests away. The facility now boasts 778 rooms, several restaurants, a spa, a gift shop, and a golf course. But even with all those amenities, a number of guests still come just to hunt for ghosts.

SAM THE BELL-GHOST

One of the Banff Springs Hotel's friendly spirits is that of Sam McCauley, a Scottish immigrant who, for many years, worked there as a bellhop. He so loved the hotel and his job there that he told coworkers that he hoped to stay and haunt the place after he died. And it seems that he may have gotten his wish. When Sam was asked to retire in the late 1970s, he became so distraught that he died soon after.

Since then, Sam's spirit has been spotted around the hotel. Shortly after his death, two female guests were locked out of their room. They asked someone to call the front desk for

help, but by the time a hotel employee arrived, the women were already in their room. They said that a friendly bellhop with white hair unlocked their door. After that, "Sam" sightings became commonplace at the Banff Springs Hotel. Some guests have reported seeing him in the hallways, while others have said that he let them into their rooms or carried their luggage. And invariably, when guests reach into their wallets to give him a tip, the kindly bellhop simply vanishes.

THE GHOST OF WEDDINGS PAST

Sam is not the only spirit to inhabit this old hotel. Another ghost that is seen there quite often is the specter of a bride who was planning to get married at the hotel shortly after it was remodeled. Because it happened so long ago, records of what happened to the poor bride no longer exist, and sources vary regarding the details. Some say that she was descending the grand staircase when her feet became entangled in the long flowing train of her gown, causing her to trip and fall down the stairs to her death. Another story suggests that the staircase was surrounded by lit candles and her dress caught on fire. In a panic, she tried to put out the fire and fell down the stairs in the process. Regardless, guests and staff members have heard strange noises coming from the bridal suite when it's empty. Many have glimpsed the bride dancing alone in the ballroom, and others have seen her descending the staircase. As they watch, her dress catches on fire, and then she suddenly disappears.

Room 873

Yet another spirit at the Banff Springs Hotel is associated with a slightly more terrifying tale. Rumors say that a family was murdered in Room 873. However, a story like this is not so good for business, so the room was eventually sealed up after guests reported seeing a child's fingerprints on the mirrors. What's so frightening about that? Well, after they are cleaned off, they mysteriously—and immediately—reappear. Visitors have also reported seeing apparitions of this poor family strolling through the halls.

Several other spirits have been reported on the property, including a bagpiper who plays for guests. You'll certainly know him if you see him because he has no head.

And then there's the helpful bartender in the Rob Roy Dining Room. Concerned about his customers' safety—and possibly their potential embarrassment—he's not afraid to tell them when they've had a bit too much to drink.

Unlike some other hotels that use their ghostly visitors to attract curious guests, the Banff Springs Hotel does not promote the possibility of paranormal activity within its walls. But judging by the tales told by former guests and staff members, it's hard to deny that something is going on there. You might just have to check in for a night...if you dare!

San Diego Ghosts Gather at the Whaley House

Even if you don't believe in ghosts, you'll be intrigued by all the chatter surrounding the Whaley House in San Diego. Famous ghost hunter Hans Holzer believed that this old family homestead might be the most haunted house in America. The U.S. Department of Commerce lists the building as an authentic Haunted House (it is one of only two structures in the country—along with the Winchester Mystery House—to hold this distinction), and the television show America's Most Haunted *called it the Most Haunted House in the United States.*

How It All Began

Built by Thomas Whaley in 1856, the Whaley House began as a one-story granary with an adjacent two-story residence. By the next year, Thomas had opened a general store on the premises. Over the years, the building also served as a county courthouse, a ballroom, a billiards hall, and a theater, among other things. Now it's a California State Historic Landmark and a museum.

Squatter's Rights

Hindsight is always 20/20, but perhaps Thomas Whaley should have thought twice about buying the property on which "Yankee Jim" Robinson was publicly hanged in 1852. After all, it was a particularly unpleasant display. The gallows were situated on the back of a wagon that was set up at the site. But being a tall man, Yankee Jim was able to reach the wagon with his feet, which delayed his death for several minutes. According to newspaper reports, when his legs were finally pulled out from under him, he "swung back and forth like a pendulum" until he died. Not a pretty sight.

Although Thomas Whaley was actually present at Yankee Jim's execution, he apparently didn't associate the property with the gruesome event that had taken place there. But soon after the house was completed, Thomas and his family began to hear heavy disembodied footsteps, as if a large man was walking through the house. Remembering what had taken place there a few years earlier, the Whaleys believed that the spirit of Yankee Jim himself was sharing their new home. Apparently, Yankee Jim was not an evil spirit because the Whaleys' youngest daughter, Lillian, lived in the house with the spirit until 1953. But to this day, visitors to the site still report hearing the heavy-footed phantom.

Family Spirits

In 1960, the house became a historic landmark and opened to the public. Since then, staff, tourists, and ghost hunters have all experienced paranormal phenomena such as apparitions, unexplained noises, and isolated cold spots. Some have even caught glimpses of a small dog running by, which just might be the spirit of the Whaleys' terrier, Dolly Varden.

Although Thomas and Anna Whaley lived in several different houses, the couple must have dearly loved their original San Diego home because they don't seem quite ready to leave it, even a century after their deaths. They have been seen—and heard—going about their daily business and doing chores in the house. Don't they know there's a cleaning service for that?

The couple has also been captured on film acting as though it was still the 1800s. Thomas was seen wandering through the house and smoking a pipe near an upstairs window, while

Anna seems to have kept up her duties as the matron of the house. People have seen her rocking a baby, tucking a child into bed, and folding clothes. Sometimes, a rocking chair is seen teetering back and forth all by itself.

Children are especially likely to see the building's former occupants. Employees frequently notice youngsters smiling or waving at people whom the adults are unable to see. And the sound of piano music that sometimes drifts through the air? Many people believe that it's Anna, still playing the tunes that she loved most in life.

Long before he became a well-known TV personality, Regis Philbin worked at a television station in San Diego. In 1964, when he and a companion paid a visit to the Whaley House to investigate the ghostly tales, Regis was startled to see the wispy figure of Anna Whaley moving along one of the walls. When he turned on a flashlight to get a better look, she disappeared, leaving only her portrait to smile back at him.

WILTED VIOLET

Thomas and Anna's daughter Violet had a particularly sad life and is thought to haunt the old house where she once lived. At the Whaley House in 1882, the beautiful Violet married a man whom her parents did not trust. Unfortunately, the marriage lasted only two weeks, after which Violet was granted a divorce. Divorce was highly uncommon in those days, and the scandal was humiliating for both Violet and her family. Violet became extremely depressed, and in 1885, she took her own life by shooting herself in the heart.

It is believed that Violet makes her presence known by turning on lights in the upstairs rooms and setting off the burglar alarm. Her spirit is also thought to be responsible for the phantom footsteps that come from the second floor and the sudden icy chills that are often felt by visitors—as though a ghost had just walked right through them.

GHOSTS GALORE

Most of the spirits at the Whaley House seem to be related to the family or the site. A young girl has been seen at several locations in and around the house. Dressed in clothing that was popular in the late 1800s, she plays with toys in the playroom, sniffs flowers in the garden, and darts in and out of the dining room very quickly. Some say that she was a playmate of the Whaley children and that she died on the property when she got tangled in a clothesline and either broke her neck or was strangled. However, there is no record of such a death occurring at the Whaley House. Others suggest that although her spirit is real, her story was made up somewhere along the way, which only adds to the intrigue of the place. As if there wasn't enough of that already!

Another female ghost seems to be attached to the part of the house that once served as a courtroom. One visitor said that as she walked into the room, she saw a woman dressed in a calico skirt, which was fashionable in the 1800s. The spirit didn't seem evil, but it didn't seem very welcoming either. The visitor captured the spectral woman's shadowy figure in a photo. It seems likely that the ghost is somehow connected to an event that took place in the courtroom.

The ghost of a man dressed in a businesslike frock coat has also appeared in the former courtroom. However, his spirit may not be strongly attached to the building because it fades away more quickly than others that are seen there.

Haunted Happenings

In addition to these apparitions, visitors, volunteers, and employees have reported other odd phenomena inside the Whaley House. Unexplained singing, organ music, and whistling have been heard, as has a toddler crying in an upstairs nursery. (This is believed to be the spirit of Thomas and Anna's son, who was also named Thomas. He died of scarlet fever at age 17 months.) Some have seen furniture levitate in the house, and others have noticed mysterious scents, such as perfume, cigar smoke, and the scent of holiday baking coming from an empty kitchen.

When visitors first enter the house, they can examine photos taken by previous guests. These images all have one thing in common: They contain mysterious objects such as shadows, orbs, and misty figures. One visitor reported trying to take photos with an otherwise reliable camera. But as soon as she tried to focus, the camera beeped, indicating that she was too close to her subject despite the fact that she was nowhere near the closest (visible) object. Once developed, the photos featured an orb or filmy shadow in nearly every shot.

At least the Whaley House spirits take some responsibility for the place. Once, after an especially long day at the museum, a staff member was getting ready to close up when all the doors and windows on both floors suddenly locked on their own, all at the same time. Sometimes, spirits just need a little alone time.

THE GHOSTLY TALES OF STEPHEN CRANE

Stephen Crane's classic Civil War novel The Red Badge of Courage is often praised for its honest and intense depiction of war. Although Crane had never experienced battle himself, war was one subject that he obviously knew something about ... another was ghosts.

BLUE LIGHT SPECIAL

In "Ghosts on the New Jersey Coast," Crane tells of the November 1854 shipwreck of the German vessel *New Era*, which was one of the worst disasters to occur on the Jersey Shore. Nearly 250 people drowned after the ship ran aground near Deal Beach and the captain and crew abandoned it, leaving the passengers at the mercy of the wind and water.

The victims were buried in a mass grave, and soon after, rumors started to spread that the dead had been buried with an untold amount of gold that they'd brought with them from Europe. However, the grave was said to be guarded by a dim blue light that floated above it and attacked anyone who tried to disturb the peaceful rest of those just below.

FIGHTING PHANTOMS

Another incident that Crane relates in "Ghosts on the New Jersey Coast" took place on the beach just south of where the famed Barnegat Lighthouse now stands. There, in 1782, a band of about 20 American sailors found an abandoned British ship run aground. The men worked all day salvaging cargo from the ship. When night fell, they were so tired that they decided to sleep on the beach. But a crew of British sailors murdered the men as they slept.

According to Crane, the hideous ghost of the British leader haunts the beach, and anyone who sleeps there will wake to find a phantom holding a knife to his or her throat. No matter how fast the person tries to run away, he or she hears the ghostly crunch of invisible footsteps right behind and knows that the evil creature is close by.

The sounds of moaning, laughter, and yelling are often faintly heard on this beach late at night. It's as if the surprise attack of long ago is being replayed.

DUTCH TREAT?

Most coastal regions have tales of ghost ships, and Crane told of New Jersey's, which is often seen in a sparsely populated area behind the Shark River near Asbury Park. The large vessel easily cruises in just inches of water and carries a crew of skeletons, whose terrifying faces look out at bystanders.

NOTHING BUT A HOUND DOG

This tale of a phantom black hound is another of Crane's scary stories. After a shipwreck, robbers waited for the dead to wash ashore so that they could steal their valuables.

Suddenly, the bandits saw a large black hound emerge from the surf. The beast was dragging the body of a man behind it. The man was lifeless, but the dog hopefully laid the body of his master on the beach and nudged him a few times.

One of the pirates saw that the man was wearing expensive jewelry. When the scavenger reached for it, the hound bared its teeth and growled, ready to defend its master. A few moments later, however, another man struck the animal with a fatal blow, and it crawled onto the body of its master to die.

But death was just the beginning for the hound. Soon after, fishermen returning home late at night saw the phantom beast on the beach. The spectral hound had blood dripping from its head and foam oozing from its mouth. His eyes blazed with demonic fire. The dog is often seen roaming along the beach with its nose down, as if trying to pick up a scent.

The Barnegat region in which this story is set is still there— a little more developed and a little more crowded but still primarily ocean and sand. It's very possible that the hound is still there too, searching for the person who did it wrong but quite possibly not caring who it encounters, as long as it's human. As Crane advised, if you come across the hound—or any of these other specters—run!

The Dark Side of the White House

From the East Wing to the West Wing, our presidential palace is reportedly one of the most haunted government buildings anywhere. That's hardly surprising given the rich history that has transpired within its walls.

The White House's First Ghost

The ghost of David Burns may be the first spirit that haunted the White House. In life, Burns donated the land on which the structure was built. One day, Franklin Roosevelt heard his name being called, and when he replied, the voice said that it was "Mr. Burns."

FDR's personal servant, Cesar Carrera, told a similar story. He was in the Yellow Oval Room when he heard a soft, distant voice say, "I'm Mr. Burns." When Cesar looked around, no one was there.

Later, when Harry Truman was president, a guard at the White House also heard a soft voice announce itself as Mr. Burns. The guard expected to see James Byrnes, Truman's secretary of state, but no one appeared. What's more, the guard checked the roster and learned that Byrnes hadn't been in the building at all that day.

William Henry Harrison Feels a Little Blue

William Henry Harrison was the first American president to die in office. While giving his inauguration address in icy, windy weather on March 4, 1841, Harrison caught a cold that quickly turned into pneumonia.

Harrison's ghost is said to wander the corridors of the White House, delirious with fever and looking for a quiet room in which to rest. Unfortunately, while Harrison's lungs filled with fluid and fever wracked his body, his doctors subjected him to painful and poisonous treatments. It is speculated that the president died not from his illness, but from the care of his doctors. Harrison passed away on April 4, 1841, just one month after taking office.

Harrison's translucent ghost is seen throughout the White House, but it is most often spotted in the residential areas. His skin is pale blue and his breathing makes an awful rattling noise. He appears to be looking for something and walks through closed doors. Some believe that he's looking for rest or a cure for his illness. Others say he's searching for his office so that he can complete his term as president.

ANDREW JACKSON LIKES THE LADIES

If you'd prefer to see a happier ghost, look for the specter of Andrew Jackson. He's often seen in the Queen's Bedroom, where his bed is on display. But Jackson may not necessarily be looking for his old bed. You see, in life, "Old Hickory" was quite the ladies' man, and today, the Queen's Bedroom is reserved for female guests of honor.

Visitors sometimes simply sense Jackson's presence in the Queen's Bedroom or feel a bone-chilling breeze when they're near his bed. Some have reported that Jackson's ghost climbs under the covers, sending guests shrieking out of the room.

Mary Todd Lincoln frequently complained about the spirit of Andrew Jackson cursing and stomping in the corridors of the White House. After she left, he stopped fussing.

OH SÉANCE CAN YOU SEE?

Séances at the White House have been nearly as numerous as the phantoms that inhabit its hallways. During a séance in the early 1860s, President Lincoln and his wife contacted the spirit of former secretary of state Daniel Webster while attempting to reach their son Willie. According to witnesses, Webster pleaded with the president to continue his efforts to end slavery. Some years later, relatives of President Ulysses S. Grant held another séance at the White House, during which they reputedly spoke with young Willie Lincoln.

In 1995—with the help of medium Jean Houston—First Lady Hillary Rodham Clinton reportedly established contact with Eleanor Roosevelt and Mahatma Gandhi. It seems some séances yield better results than others. Describing her fascination with White House spirits, Clinton said, "There is something about the house at night that you just feel like you are summoning up the spirits of all the people who have lived there and worked there and walked through the halls there."

Ghosts of Presidents' Families and Foes

Abigail Adams used to hang laundry on clotheslines in the White House's East Room. Her ghost appears there regularly wearing a cap and wrapped in a shawl. She's usually carrying laundry or checking to see if her laundry is dry.

The spirit of Dolley Madison defends the Rose Garden that she designed and planted. When Woodrow Wilson's wife Edith ordered staff members to dig up the garden to plant new flowers, Dolley's apparition allegedly insisted that no one was going to touch her roses. The landscaping ceased, and today, Dolley's roses remain exactly as they were when the Madisons lived in the White House in the early 1800s.

After Abraham Lincoln's son Willie died in February 1862 following a brief illness, the president became obsessed with his son's death and had his coffin reopened at least twice, just to look at him. Willie's apparition has been seen at the White House regularly since his death, most often manifesting in the bedrooms on the second floor, where his ghost was once witnessed by Lyndon Johnson's daughter Lynda.

Other spirits also seem to like that room. Harry Truman's mother died there and may have made her presence known afterward. Lynda used to report hearing unexplained footsteps in the bedroom. And sometimes, her phone would ring in the middle of the night. But when she answered, no one was on the line.

Also on the second floor, people have heard the ghost of Frances Cleveland crying, perhaps reliving the time when her husband, Grover, was diagnosed with cancer.

One very out-of-place spirit seems to be that of a British soldier from around 1814, when the White House was besieged and burned during the War of 1812. The uniformed specter looks lost and holds a torch. When he realizes that he's been spotted, he becomes alarmed and vanishes.

"Now about those ghosts. I'm sure they're here and I'm not half so alarmed at meeting up with any of them as I am at having to meet the live nuts I have to see every day."

—First Lady Bess Truman

THE HOOSAC TUNNEL

By the mid-1800s, the train was the most popular form of transportation in America, and competition between railroad lines was fierce. If a means could be found to shorten a route, create a link, or speed up a journey, it was generally taken to help ensure the railroad's continued profitability.

In 1848, the newly formed Troy and Greenfield Railroad proposed a direct route that would link Greenfield and

Williamstown, Massachusetts. In Williamstown, the line would connect to an existing route on which trains could travel to Troy, New York, and points west. The time-saving measure seemed like a brilliant move, except for one not-so-small detail: Between Greenfield and Williamstown stood the forbidding Hoosac Mountain. In order to tame it, the railroad would need to drill a tunnel—but at nearly five miles in length, it would have to be the world's *longest* tunnel.

THE GREAT BORE

In 1851, the project was set in motion. Almost immediately, trouble arose when drillers learned that the soft rock through which they were supposed to be boring was, in fact, harder than nails. In 1861, funding dried up, and by 1862, the Troy and Greenfield Railroad had defaulted on its loan. The state of Massachusetts stepped in to complete the tunnel.

With a steady stream of cash and a government bent on completing the project, the Hoosac Tunnel was officially opened in 1876. The project had taken a quarter century to complete at a total cost of $21 million. Nearly 200 lives were lost while the tunnel was built, with 13 being the result of an incident that's legendary to this day.

TRAGEDY STRIKES

The tragic event took place on October 17, 1867, inside the tunnel's central shaft—a vertical hole that was drilled from atop the mountain to intersect with the tunnel 1,028 feet below. The purpose of the shaft was to supply much-needed ventilation to the tunnel.

On this particular day, the shaft reached into the mountain some 538 feet. While attempting to light a lamp, a worker accidentally ignited a gasoline tank. Within seconds, an inferno rocketed up to the surface, destroying the pumping station and hoist house located above, causing them to collapse into the deep pit. Unfortunately, 13 men were working in the shaft during the incident. As soon as was humanly possible, a miner was lowered into the smoldering cavity to search for survivors. He passed out during the long trip but managed to gasp "no hope" upon his return to the surface.

Without an operational pump, the cavity eventually filled to the brim with seepage and rainwater. It wasn't until a year later that the central shaft gave up its grisly contents. As it turns out, most of the victims hadn't died from the flames or from drowning. The stranded men had built a survival raft but were slowly suffocated by the poisonous gases and the smoke from the oxygen-hungry flames raging above them.

SPIRITS RISE

In a 1985 article, Glenn Drohan—a reporter for the *North Adams Transcript*—told of strange phenomena at the tunnel, such as "vague shapes and muffled wails near the water-filled pit." Shortly after the accident occurred, workmen allegedly saw the spirits of the lost miners carrying picks and shovels. The workers called out to the missing men, but they did not answer, and their apparitions quickly vanished.

Other tragic goings-on at the Hoosac Tunnel include the strange death of Ringo Kelley. In 1865, when explosive nitroglycerin was first used for excavation, Kelley, Billy Nash, and Ned Brinkman attempted to set a charge of nitro before running for cover. But Kelley somehow set off the explosion prematurely, burying his coworkers in the process.

Soon after, Ringo Kelley vanished. He was not seen again until March 30, 1866, when his lifeless body was found two miles inside the tunnel. Bizarrely, he had been strangled to death at the precise spot where Nash and Brinkman had died. Investigators never had any leads, but workmen had an ominous feeling about Kelley's demise. They believed that the vengeful spirits of Nash and Brinkman had done him in.

PRESENT-DAY POLTERGEISTS

The tunnel also features its share of hauntings from the more recent past, including railroad worker Joseph Impoco's trio of supernatural tales. In an article that appeared in *The Berkshire Sampler* on October 30, 1977, Impoco told reporter Eileen Kuperschmid that he was chipping ice from the tracks one day when he heard a voice say, "Run, Joe, run!" As Impoco tells it, "I turned, and sure enough, there was No. 60 coming at me. Boy, did I jump back fast! When I looked [back], there was no one there."

Six weeks later, Impoco was working with an iron crowbar, doing his best to free cars that were stuck to the icy tracks. Suddenly, he heard, "Joe! Joe! Drop it, Joe!" He instinctively dropped the crowbar just as 11,000 volts of electricity struck it from a short-circuited power line overhead.

In another incident, Impoco was removing trees from the tunnel's entrance when, from out of nowhere, an enormous oak fell directly toward him. He managed to outrun the falling tree, but he heard a frightening, ethereal laugh as he ran. He was certain that it hadn't come from any of his coworkers.

TRAVEL TIPS

For the brave at heart, a visit to the Hoosac Tunnel can prove awe-inspiring and educational. The tunnel is still used, so walking inside it is strictly off-limits, but a well-worn path beside the tracks leads to the tunnel's entrance. For those who are looking to avoid things that go bump in the night, a trip to the nearby North Adams' Hoosac Tunnel Museum in Western Gateway Heritage State Park will reveal the incredible history of this five-mile-long portal into another dimension—and will do so far away from Ringo Kelley's haunts. All aboard!

A Host of Ghosts Haunt the White Eagle Saloon

The building that's now the White Eagle Saloon in Portland, Oregon, has been many things since it was constructed in the early 1900s, including a hotel, a rooming house, and, most recently, a tavern that features live music. For much of its history, it has also been haunted.

Over the years, a great deal of paranormal activity has been reported at the White Eagle Saloon. Most of it has been harmless—but not all of it. For example, many years ago, a waitress was walking to the basement after closing to add up the day's receipts when something unseen shoved her down the stairs. The woman's hysterical screams got the attention of the bartender and doorman. When they came to her aid, they had a bucket hurled at them by an invisible force. Not surprisingly, the waitress quit the next day.

To date, this is the most violent outburst from the spirits at the White Eagle Saloon. But many other harmless events that simply defy explanation have occurred there.

Weirdness in the Bathroom

One of the saloon's ghosts seems to enjoy flushing the toilet in the men's room. Many people have observed this unusual phenomenon, usually after closing. Is it a faulty toilet? No way, says owner Chuck Hughes—the flushing has occurred with two different toilets, and it is sometimes joined by the sound of footsteps in the hallway outside the restroom.

Chuck has experienced quite a few unexplained events over the years. For example, one day he was removing a lock from a door on the second floor when he heard what sounded like a woman crying at the other end of the hallway. But as he walked toward the source of the noise, the crying ceased. Chuck checked all the rooms on the second floor but found nothing. When he returned to his work on the door, the crying began again. Chuck again tried to find the source of the sound, and this time, he felt an overwhelming chill.

Frightened, Chuck rushed downstairs and exited the tavern. Looking back at the building, he saw what he later described as a ghostly shape in one of the windows on the second floor. After moving to the back of the building, Chuck saw the same specter at another window. Shaken, he refused to go upstairs again for nearly a year.

A Ghost Named Sam

It is believed that one of the ghosts haunting the White Eagle Saloon is a former employee named Sam, who some say was adopted at a young age by one of the building's early owners. A burly guy, Sam lived and worked at the White Eagle until his death in the 1930s.

After Sam died in his room at the White Eagle, his body was removed and his room was locked and left pretty much the way it was for a long time. Is Sam still hanging around the tavern? Many believe so. Chuck Hughes recalls that after he bought the White Eagle, the door to Sam's room would not stay open. Time after time, the door was left open, only to be found shut—and locked—a couple of days later. Apparently, Sam likes his privacy.

Chuck says that he's experienced enough unexplained phenomena at the White Eagle to fill a book. For example, he used to keep a bed in the basement to use when he worked late. One night, he awoke to find himself being nudged by invisible hands. This freaked him out, so he got dressed and went home.

While working in the basement after hours, Chuck often heard voices and footsteps above him. Sometimes the voices even called his name. But every time he went to investigate, no one was there.

SUSPECTED SPOOKS

The White Eagle Saloon has hosted its share of wild times and even wilder characters over the years, so it's no surprise that it's haunted. Sam is believed to be the spook that flushes the men's room toilet, and the crying woman may be the spirit of one of the many people who worked there long ago.

But who pushed the waitress down the cellar stairs? Some suspect that it was the ghost of a former bouncer who was known for harshly treating the women who worked there.

One day, the guy simply disappeared. Was he murdered? If so, that might explain why his angry spirit is still attached to the White Eagle.

Lingering Spirits of the Eastland Disaster

The city of Chicago has a dark history of disaster and death involving devastating fires, horrific accidents, and catastrophic events. One of the most tragic incidents took place on July 24, 1915. On that overcast afternoon, hundreds of people died in the Chicago River when the Eastland *capsized just a few feet from the dock. This event left a ghostly imprint on the Windy City that is still felt today.*

Company Picnic Turns Tragic

July 24 was going to be a special day for thousands of Chicagoans. It was the date of the annual summer picnic for employees of the Western Electric Company, which was to be held across Lake Michigan in Michigan City, Indiana. Officials at the utility company had encouraged workers to bring along friends and relatives, but they were surprised when more than 7,000 people arrived to be transported across the lake on the five boats chartered for the day. Three of the steamers—the *Theodore Roosevelt*, the *Petoskey*, and the *Eastland*—were docked on the Chicago River near Clark Street.

The *Eastland* had a reputation for top-heaviness and instability, and on this fateful morning, the boat was filled to its limit. In addition, a new law passed as a result of the *Titanic* tragedy required that the boat be equipped with more lifeboats. This made the ship even more unstable than it already was. Basically, it was a recipe for disaster.

DEATH AND THE *EASTLAND*

As passengers boarded the *Eastland*, the boat began rocking back and forth, so the crew made adjustments to provide more stability. As the boat was preparing to depart, some passengers went below deck, hoping to warm up on the cool, cloudy morning. But many on the overcrowded steamer jammed onto the deck to wave to onlookers on shore. The *Eastland* tilted once again, but this time more severely, and passengers began to panic. Moments later, the *Eastland* rolled onto its side, coming to rest at the bottom of the river, 18 feet below the surface. One side of the boat was still above water in some spots.

Passengers on the deck were tossed into the river, splashing about in a mass of bodies. The overturned boat created a current that pulled some of the floundering swimmers to their doom, and many of the women's

long dresses were snagged on the ship, tugging them down to the bottom.

Those inside were thrown to one side of the ship when it capsized. Heavy furniture onboard crushed some passengers, and those who were not killed instantly drowned a few moments later when water rushed inside. A few managed to escape, but most didn't. Their bodies were later found trapped in a tangled heap.

Firefighters and volunteers soon arrived and tried to help people escape through portholes. They also cut holes in the part of the boat that was above the water line. Approximately 1,660 passengers survived the disaster, but they still ended up in the river. Many onlookers jumped in or threw life preservers, as well as ropes, boxes, and anything that floated, into the water to help the panicked and drowning passengers.

In the end, 844 people died, many of them young women and children. No clear explanation was officially given for why the vessel capsized.

The bodies of those who perished in the tragedy were wrapped in sheets and placed on the *Theodore Roosevelt* or lined up along the docks. Department stores sent wagons to carry the dead to hospitals, funeral homes, and makeshift morgues, such as the Second Regiment Armory where more than 200 bodies were sent.

After the ship was removed from the river, it was sold and later became a U.S. warship renamed the U.S.S. *Wilmette*. The ship never saw any action, but it was used as a training vessel during World War II. After the war, it was decommissioned, and in 1947, it was scrapped.

LINGERING SPIRITS

The *Eastland* may be gone, but its story and ghosts continue to linger nearly a century later. At the time of the incident, the Second Regiment Armory was the only public building large enough to be used as a temporary morgue. Chicagoans with missing loved ones filed through, searching for familiar faces. In 22 cases, there was no one left to identify them—those families were completely wiped out. The names of these victims were learned from neighbors who came searching for their friends. The weeping, crying, and moaning of the bereaved echoed off the walls of the armory for days.

As years passed, the armory building went through several incarnations before it was purchased by Harpo Studios, the production company owned by talk-show host Oprah Winfrey. A number of *Oprah Winfrey Show* staff members, security guards, and maintenance workers believed that the studio was haunted by the spirits of those who tragically lost their lives on the *Eastland*. Many employees experienced unexplained phenomena, including the sighting of a woman in a long gray dress who walks the corridors and then vanishes into the walls. Some believe she is the spirit of a mourner who came to the armory looking for her family and left a bit of herself behind at the place where she felt her greatest sense of loss. Staff members also witnessed doors opening and closing on their own and heard sobbing sounds and phantom footsteps on the lobby staircase.

Chicago River Ghosts

In the same way that the former armory seems to have been imprinted with a ghostly recording of past events, the Chicago River seems to be haunted too. For years, people walking on the Clark Street Bridge have heard crying and moaning coming from the river. Some have witnessed the apparitions of victims splashing in the water. On several occasions, witnesses have called the police for help. One man even jumped into the river to save what he thought was a person drowning. When he returned to the surface, he discovered that he had been in the water alone. He had no explanation for what he'd seen, other than to admit that it might have been a ghost.

So it seems that the horror of the *Eastland* disaster has left its mark on these spots and continues to replay itself, ensuring that the *Eastland* victims will never be forgotten.

THE "GREY LADY" OF EVANSVILLE, INDIANA

The Willard Library in Evansville, Indiana, has a long history of supernatural activity. But while multiple ghosts typically inhabit many haunted buildings, only one spirit seems to roam the stacks at this old Victorian library—an entity known as "the Lady in Grey."

NOT SHY AT ALL

According to local reports, the Lady in Grey has been haunting the Willard Library since at least the 1930s. The first known encounter with her occurred in 1937, when a janitor ran into the lonely ghost as he entered the library's cellar to stoke the furnace. There, he saw a mysterious woman dressed all in gray. A veil was draped from her face to her shoes, and she glowed ethereally in the darkness.

That may have been the first confirmed encounter with the Grey Lady, but it certainly wasn't the last. In fact, according to library employees and patrons, this spirit seems to go out of her way to make her presence known.

On one occasion, the members of a local genealogy group noticed the distinct scent of perfume in the library's research room. None of the group members was wearing perfume at the time, and no one else had entered the room while they were there.

Margaret Maier, who worked at the library for more than four decades, also smelled the Grey Lady's musky perfume at her own home. Maier speculated that the spirit briefly followed her home while the library was being renovated. In addition to the scent of perfume, Maier and her sister reported feeling an unseen presence in their midst, as well as an inexplicable chill at Maier's home.

SPOOKY SHENANIGANS

She clearly means no harm, but the Lady in Grey isn't above playing pranks on library staffers. One night, Bettye Elaine Miller, who was head librarian from 1972 to 1975, was working late when she heard water running on the second floor. She rushed upstairs to find that a bathroom faucet had been mysteriously turned on. Later, another librarian who was using the same bathroom watched in horror as a faucet turned on by itself.

Over the years, reports of paranormal activity at the Willard Library have become so commonplace that, with the library's permission, the *Evansville Courier & Press* installed three Internet-connected "ghost cams" in the building so that curious ghost hunters can try to catch a glimpse of the Grey Lady. The cameras have proven quite popular with fans of the paranormal, logging hundreds of thousands of hits since they first went online. Visit LibraryGhost.com to check it out for yourself.

A Ghost Revealed

Of course, everyone wants to know the identity of the mysterious Grey Lady. Local historians believe that she is the ghost of Louise Carpenter, the daughter of Willard Carpenter, the man who the library is named after. According to reports, Louise was very unhappy with the fact that in his will, her father left a great deal of his money for the construction of a public library. She even tried to sue the library's board of trustees, claiming that her father was not mentally fit when he wrote his will.

Louise's lawsuit was unsuccessful, and she was unable to stop the library's construction. A theory among many ghost hunters suggests that, upon her death in 1908, Louise's spirit came to reside within the library and will stay there until the property is returned to the Carpenter family, which is quite unlikely.

Libraries are popular haunts for ghosts, but few have logged as many reputable sightings and paranormal occurrences as the Willard Library. It very well may be the most haunted library in the United States, thanks to a gray-clad spirit that still holds a grudge, even from beyond the grave.

Unsettled Spirits at the Sanatorium

It was designed to save lives at a time when an epidemic was sweeping the nation. Little did its developers know that they were erecting a building in which scores of people would take their last gasping breaths. Is it any wonder that the halls of the Waverly Hills Sanatorium still echo with the footsteps of those who died there?

Origins

In the early 1900s, an outbreak of tuberculosis (TB) spread across the United States. In an effort to stop the highly contagious disease from spreading, TB sanatoriums and hospitals were built. In 1910, a small, two-story facility known as the Waverly Hills Sanatorium opened in Louisville, Kentucky. It could house nearly 50 patients.

They Just Keep Coming...

Without a cure or even a way to slow the disease, little could be done for TB patients at the time. Treatment often consisted of nothing more than exposure to fresh air and heat lamps.

The sanatorium was expanded in the 1920s as more and more patients were brought there. After the renovations, Waverly Hills became a massive five-story structure that could house nearly 400 patients. But once again, the rooms quickly filled up. The only thing that kept the facility from overcrowding was the fact that, without a cure, many of the patients passed away. Just how many people died there is unknown—some estimates go as high as 65,000. In truth, the number is probably closer to 8,000, but that's still a staggering number when you consider that tuberculosis causes patients to slowly and painfully waste away over the course of weeks or even months.

In the 1940s, treatments for TB were introduced, and as a result, the number of patients at Waverly Hills consistently declined until the facility was officially shut down in 1961.

THE FINAL YEARS

A short time later, Waverly Hills was reopened as the Woodhaven Geriatric Center. This chapter of the building's history came to an end around 1980 amid whispers of cruelty and abuse toward the patients. Before long, those rumors became full-blown urban legends involving torturous treatments such as electroshock therapy. Not surprisingly, it wasn't long before people started saying that the abandoned, foreboding structure was haunted.

MEET THE GHOSTS

So who are the ghosts that are said to haunt Waverly Hills? Sadly, the identities of most of them are unknown, but many have been encountered. Almost every floor of the building has hosted paranormal activity, such as disembodied voices and ghostly footsteps. Doors have been known to open and close by themselves, and bits of debris have been thrown at unsuspecting visitors. It is said that all you have to do is wait quietly to spot one of the many shadow people that walk down the hallways. Of course, if you're looking for a more interactive encounter, you can always head up to the third floor. There, you might find the spirit of a young girl in the solarium. If she's not there, check the staircases nearby— apparently she likes to run up and down them.

Waverly Hills is also home to the ghost of a young boy who likes to play with a small ball that sometimes appears on the floor. Not wanting to wait to find the ball, some visitors have brought their own, which they leave in a certain spot, only to see it roll away or even vanish before it appears on a different floor altogether.

WELCOME TO ROOM 502

Of all the allegedly haunted areas at Waverly Hills, none holds a candle to Room 502. Most of the stories associated with the room center on two nurses, both of whom supposedly committed suicide on the premises. One nurse is said to have killed herself there in 1928. Apparently, she was a single woman who discovered that she was pregnant. Feeling that she had nowhere to turn, the young woman decided to hang herself. The other nurse who worked in Room 502 is said to have killed herself in 1932 by jumping from the roof, although the reason why is unclear. No proof of either of these suicides has been unearthed, but that has not stopped visitors to Room 502 from experiencing paranormal activity. Upon entering the room, people often report feeling "heavy" or the sensation of being watched. It is quite common for guests to witness shadow figures darting around the room, and occasionally, a lucky visitor catches a glimpse of a spectral nurse standing by the window.

THE BODY CHUTE

When the building was expanded in the 1920s, a rather morbid part of the sanatorium was constructed: the Body Chute—a 500-foot-long underground tunnel leading from the main building to a nearby road and a set of railroad tracks. Some believe that the tunnel was created for convenience, while others think it was designed to prevent patients from seeing the truth—that many of them were dying. Although it was called the Body Chute, bodies were never dumped into it. Instead, they were carried through it on gurneys. The tunnel was even equipped with a motorized cable system to help with transportation.

People walking through the Body Chute have reported hearing disembodied voices, whispering, and even painful groans. And sometimes, shadow figures are seen wandering through the tunnel. But because the only light down there comes from random air vents, the figures vanish almost as quickly as they appear.

Lights, Camera, Ghosts!

After the TV show *Scariest Places on Earth* featured Waverly Hills in a 2001 episode, numerous programs began filming at the sanatorium. *Ghost Hunters* visited there twice—once in 2006 and again in 2007 as part of its annual live Halloween investigation. *Most Haunted* came all the way from the UK in 2008, and *Ghost Adventures* spent a night locked inside the sanatorium in 2010. But of all the episodes filmed at Waverly Hills, none was more bizarre than that of the short-lived VH1 show *Celebrity Paranormal Project.*

The debut episode of the series was shot at Waverly Hills and aired in October 2006. It featured comedian Hal Sparks, actor Gary Busey, *Survivor* winner Jenna Morasca, model Toccara Jones, and model/actress Donna D'Errico conducting an investigation. The supernatural activity began early in the evening, shortly after Busey and Morasca were sent to Room 418 to investigate. They weren't there long before their thermal-imaging camera picked up shapes moving around the room and even sitting on a bed near them. When Morasca was left in the room alone, she heard all sorts of strange noises and even encountered a small red ball that wasn't there when the pair first entered the room.

When Sparks was in the solarium, he rolled balls across the floor in an attempt to convince the spirits to play with him. The footage shows what appears to be one of the balls rolling back to him. At around the same time, Sparks reported seeing a small black shape—like that of a child—run past the doorway. Later in the evening, D'Errico heard the sound of footsteps and reported feeling that someone was following her. She also heard what sounded like people screaming. She was so frightened that she ran away from the building in terror. When she rejoined the other investigators, she said that she had seen the figure of a man standing in a hallway.

The evening ended with the entire group attempting to contact the spirits in Room 502. As they asked questions, banging noises and footsteps were heard coming from all around them. When they left the building, they were still hearing noises, and they encountered a child's ball that seemed to appear from out of nowhere.

"COME JOIN US"

Waverly Hills Sanatorium is open for tours, both during the day and for overnight ghost hunts. Just be assured that no matter how many ghosts inhabit Waverly Hills, there is always room for more.

More Haunted Restaurants

The next time you enjoy a meal at your favorite restaurant, know that you may be dining with some unseen guests. Here are a few eateries where a ghostly good time is always on the menu.

Stone's Public House (Ashland, Massachusetts)

Since 1834, Stone's Public House has been serving up food and drinks. Should you stop in for a bite, take a good look at the photo of John Stone that hangs over the restaurant's fireplace so that you'll be able to recognize his ghost when it appears. Stone's spirit is said to be one of a handful that haunts the pub. Other resident ghosts include that of a man who Stone accidentally murdered in an argument over a card game. Stone and several friends allegedly buried the man in the basement and have been condemned to spend eternity haunting the scene of the crime along with their victim. The spirits make their presence known by breaking glasses, causing cold breezes, and appearing as shadow figures.

Vino's Brewpub (Little Rock, Arkansas)

Vino's is a brewery, a pizza parlor, and a great place to hear live music. After the place opened in 1990, it attracted a following among the living—but it has quite a group of non-living fans too. The source of the haunting is unknown, but employees say that the building has a creepy vibe. It features several spots that are permanently cold for no scientific reason and other cold spots that move around. Banging, thumps, and creaking noises are heard in parts of the building that appear to be empty. And after closing, staff members stack up the chairs to mop the floors and then leave them that way overnight. But when employees arrive the next day, they often find the chairs scattered around the restaurant.

Historic White Horse Inn (Metamora, Michigan)

Advertised as "Michigan's Oldest Restaurant," the White Horse Inn has been in business since 1850, when Lorenzo Hoard opened Hoard House to serve hungry and weary travelers. Lorenzo is believed to be one of the building's many ghosts. He typically waits upstairs until the restaurant becomes lively. Then he makes his presence known by causing lights to flicker or trays to crash to the floor. Patrons and staff members acknowledge his presence by saying, "Hey Lorenzo!"

Orbs are common in photos taken at the restaurant. And sometimes, in an antique mirror in the hallway, Lorenzo can be seen smiling next to a living person's reflection. Doors that are left closed overnight are found open in the morning. And each night, the owners leave Lorenzo's boots at the top of the stairs—just in case he wants to check out the town overnight. Staff members have heard heavy footsteps clomping around above them late at night when no one else is in the building, and some mornings, Lorenzo's boots have mysteriously moved to another location.

COUNTRY HOUSE RESTAURANT (STONY BROOK, NEW YORK)

Like many haunted eateries, the Country House Restaurant occupies a former residence with a troubled past. The structure was originally built in 1710. During the Revolutionary War, the family who owned the house fled for New Jersey and left a woman named Annette Williamson in charge of the property. Soon after, British soldiers occupied the house, and Annette was killed. It is unclear whether she was killed by the British because they thought she was a spy or if she was killed by her neighbors, who accused anyone who didn't fight the British of working for them.

Either way, Annette's spirit lingers at her former home. Many people have seen her looking out the window of the room in which she was reportedly killed, but she typically hangs out in the kitchen and by the stairs. When she's around, unexplainable footsteps can be heard and objects seem to move on their own. Annette's apparition has blonde hair and blue eyes, and she wears a white Colonial-style dress. She is generally friendly, and children at the restaurant often ask their parents if they can play with the pretty young woman. But don't get on her bad side—she once threw a glass of wine in a skeptic's face!

Stephen Decatur's Ghost

In Washington, D.C., a sullen figure stands at a window, looking at the world outside—even though he is a visitor from the Great Beyond. The figure is the ghost of Stephen Decatur, one of the country's greatest military heroes—long dead but condemned to prowl the halls of his former home.

Rising Star

In 1807, Stephen Decatur was already a war hero for the young United States. He had received recognition for his bravery against the Barbary Pirates and for serving as a member of a naval commission that investigated the actions of Commodore James Barron. Barron was the commander of the U.S. frigate *Chesapeake*. After the British ship *Leopold* fired a shot across the *Chesapeake*'s bow, Barron boarded the *Leopold* and took four of its sailors into custody. At the time, tensions between Great Britain and America were running high, so a commission was organized to investigate Barron's actions. It found that Barron had not received permission for his actions, so he was court-martialed and suspended for five years. Decatur spoke against Barron at the hearing, and Barron was not a man to forgive and forget.

When the War of 1812 broke out between the United States and England, Decatur took command of the *Chesapeake* and built up his reputation while Barron seethed on the sidelines. Then, in 1818, Decatur and his wife, Susan, became power players on the Washington, D.C., social scene after they built a house on fashionable Lafayette Square. However, Decatur's past would come back to haunt him. Over the years, Barron had unleashed a series of personal attacks on him. The whole affair culminated in early 1820 when Barron challenged Decatur to a duel.

FALLING STAR

The night before the duel, Decatur stared glumly from his bedroom window, looking at his estate and the neighborhood. The next day, at a field in Maryland, Decatur—apparently taking a cue from Alexander Hamilton—attempted only to wound Barron (even though Decatur was an expert marksman). However, Barron—taking a page from Aaron Burr's playbook—shot to kill and mortally wounded his enemy. Decatur was carried home, where he died an agonizing death on March 22, 1820. While he lay dying, his heartbroken wife, Susan, could barely look at him because she was so upset.

ETERNAL STAR

Soon after his death, people began seeing a figure staring sadly out of the window where Decatur himself had stood on the night before the duel. The ghost was seen so often that eventually the window was sealed up. But bricks and mortar can't keep a good ghost down—Decatur's apparition continued to manifest throughout the house and at other windows.

Today, the former Decatur home is a museum of White House history. However, that has not stopped the ghost of Stephen Decatur from roaming its halls and appearing in various rooms, always with an expression of utter sadness on his face.

Sometimes, in the early morning hours, a figure is spotted leaving the building through the back door. It carries a black box—perhaps containing a dueling pistol—just as Decatur did on the last day of his life. Inside the house, people have felt unbelievable sadness and emptiness in the first-floor room where Decatur died.

However, Stephen Decatur is not the only restless spirit that haunts the Lafayette Square property. Disembodied sobbing and wailing have been heard throughout the house. Some speculate that it's the ghost of Susan Decatur reliving the time of her life's greatest sorrow.

"The boundaries which divide life from death are at best shadowy and vague. Who shall say where the one ends and the other begins."

—Edgar Allan Poe, "The Premature Burial"

Tombstone Shadows

In its heyday, Tombstone, Arizona, was known as "the town too tough to die." Apparently, its ghosts like that nickname because there are so many spirits roaming its streets that Tombstone is a strong contender for the title of "Most Haunted Town in America." Here are a few of the most notable phantoms that still call this Wild West town home.

Virgil Earp

A man in a long black coat stands on a sidewalk in Tombstone. The people who see him assume that he's an actor in this former rough-and-tumble Wild West town. But as he starts to walk across the street, a strange thing happens—he vanishes in mid-stride. Only then do people realize that they've just seen one of the many ghosts that haunt this legendary town.

It is usually assumed that the man in the black coat is the ghost of U.S. Deputy Marshal Virgil Earp, who may be reliving one of his life's darkest moments. On December 28, 1881, he was shot and wounded when he was ambushed by outlaws who were seeking revenge for the infamous Gunfight at the O.K. Corral two months prior. Virgil survived the attack, but his left arm was permanently maimed.

Morgan Earp

In March 1882, another group of outlaws—who were also out for revenge for the Gunfight at the O.K. Corral—gunned down Morgan Earp, the brother of noted lawmen Virgil and

Wyatt Earp. Morgan was shot in the back and killed while playing pool. Some say that you can still hear his dying words whispered at the location where he was murdered.

BIG NOSE KATE

Big Nose Kate was the girlfriend of gunslinger Doc Holliday, who was a friend of the Earps. Her ghost is reportedly responsible for the footsteps and whispered words that are heard at the Crystal Palace Saloon. Lights there turn on and off by themselves, and gambling wheels sometimes spin for no reason, causing speculation that, just as in life, Kate still prefers the company of rowdy men.

SWAMPER

Big Nose Kate's Saloon was originally the Grand Hotel, and a man known as Swamper used to work there as a handyman. He lived in the basement, not far from some of the town's silver mines. When he wasn't working, Swamper dug a tunnel to one of the mines and began increasing his income with silver nuggets.

After all the effort that he'd put in, Swamper was not about to let go of his silver so easily—not even after he died. He reportedly haunts Big Nose Kate's Saloon. Perhaps he's still hanging around to protect his loot, which has never been found. Naturally, he's often spotted in the basement, but he also likes to show up in photos taken by visitors.

THE BIRD CAGE THEATRE

Anyplace where 26 people were violently killed is almost certain to be a spectral smorgasbord. Such is the case with Tombstone's infamously wild Bird Cage Theatre.

One of the most frequently seen apparitions at the Bird Cage is that of a man who carries a clipboard and wears striped pants and a card-dealer's visor. He's been known to appear on stage, glide across it, and then walk through a wall. Visitors have complimented the management on how authentic the Wild West costumes look only to be told that nobody at the Bird Cage dresses in period clothing.

One night long after closing time, an employee watched a misty woman in white walk slowly through the cellar. And although smoking and drinking are not allowed at the Bird Cage, the scents of cigar smoke and whiskey still linger there. Visitors also hear unexplained sounds, such as a woman singing, a female sighing, glasses clinking, and cards shuffling, as if the ghosts are trying to finish a game that's gone on for far too long.

NELLIE CASHMAN'S RESTAURANT

Nellie Cashman's is another haunted hot spot in Tombstone. Patrons at the eatery report hearing strange noises and seeing dishes suddenly crash to the floor. The ghosts at Nellie's have no patience for skeptics. A patron who made fun of all things supernatural found herself wearing the contents of a mustard container that inexplicably leaped off a table.

FRED WHITE

Of the many deaths in Tombstone during the days of the Wild West, one of the most tragic was that of town marshal Fred White. In October 1880, Fred was trying to arrest "Curly Bill" Brocius when Bill's gun accidentally went off. Fred was killed right there on the street, and his ghost is rumored to haunt the site, apparently still angry with the way his life was so abruptly taken from him.

BOOTHILL GRAVEYARD

It would almost seem impossible if Tombstone's legendary Boothill Graveyard wasn't haunted. But not to worry—the final resting place of so many who were violently taken from this life is said to harbor many restless spirits, including that of Billy Clanton, one of the victims of the Gunfight at the O.K. Corral. Billy's apparition has been seen rising from his grave and walking toward town. Strange lights and sounds are also said to come from the cemetery.

GEORGE BUFORD

Violent deaths came in all forms in Tombstone. One of those occurred when a man named George Buford shot his girl-friend and then himself. Apparently, his aim was better the second time because she lived, but he died. George is said to haunt the building where he once lived, which is now a bed-and-breakfast. His spirit has been seen in and around the building. Random lights also appear there for no reason, and the doorbell sometimes rings on its own in the middle of the night. It seems that ghostly George hasn't lost his fondness for the ladies either. Women in the house have felt their hair being stroked and sensed someone touching the backs of their necks. Of course, when they turn around, no one is there.

THE ANGRY SPIRITS OF THE OLD SLAVE HOUSE

Slave trading was never legal in Illinois. When it became a state in 1818, it did so as a free state. But that did not stop John Hart Crenshaw of Equality, Illinois, from kidnapping free black men and women and turning them into slaves. That was in the 1830s and '40s, but it seems that the spirits of the people Crenshaw abused are resting anything but peacefully in the house known as Hickory Hill.

NOT EXACTLY THE SALT OF THE EARTH

John Hart Crenshaw built his empire mining salt. Today, salt is primarily used as a seasoning, but before refrigeration, salt had many uses. It was a valuable product that was sometimes even used in place of money.

In the 1800s, working in the salt mines was difficult, dangerous, and physically exhausting. Crenshaw owned several salt mines in southern Illinois, but he had trouble finding people to work there. Fortunately for him, even though slavery was illegal in Illinois, a quirk in the law allowed slaves to be *leased* (or rented) in the county where his mines were located. And so Crenshaw began leasing slaves so that he would always have a steady supply of workers. But that wasn't enough for Crenshaw, so he started kidnapping free black men and women and runaway slaves. Some of them he put to work in his mines, others he sold into slavery.

Over time, Crenshaw became a wealthy man. In 1817, he had married Sinia Taylor, and in the early 1830s, he began building a proper home for her. The three-story house that he called Hickory Hill was built high on a hill and had massive columns out front. However, the most important feature of the house was not easily seen. A secret passageway actually allowed wagons to bring their cargo of slaves directly into the house. The property also reputedly included a secret tunnel that connected the home's basement to the nearby Saline River. This was used to unload slaves brought there by boat and get them into the house without being seen.

Once inside the house, Crenshaw's human cargo was led up a narrow flight of stairs to the third floor, where they were chained inside tiny, dirty spaces smaller than closets. A whipping post occupied a prominent place nearby.

There on the almost airless third floor, Crenshaw kept the people who he would either put to work in his mines or sell into slavery. Not content with just stealing human beings, Crenshaw also began a breeding program. One slave named "Uncle Bob" allegedly fathered 300 children.

WE'RE ON TO YOU...

In 1842, Crenshaw was arrested for arranging the kidnapping of a free black woman and her children. He went to court, but unfortunately, the prosecuting attorney couldn't prove the charges, and Crenshaw was set free.

But soon after, rumors began to circulate about Crenshaw's business activities. These rumblings, combined with the earlier charges, upset many local residents. In March 1842, one of Crenshaw's steam mills burned to the ground. It was believed that a group of free black men (who were fed up with Crenshaw's actions) took matters into their own hands.

In 1846, Crenshaw's business began to fail as demand for Illinois salt started to decline. After he was attacked by one of his employees (which resulted in him losing a leg), Crenshaw closed down most of his salt operations.

ATTIC ANTICS

John Hart Crenshaw died in 1871. In 1913, the Sisk family purchased his house, and later, in the mid-1920s, they started giving tours of the home. Considering the evil and human suffering that took place at Hickory Hill (aka "the

Old Slave House"), it is no surprise that the building is haunted. Visitors have often heard disembodied moans, cries, and whispers coming from the third floor. Rattling chains have also been heard, as have the shuffling of feet and the soft sounds of comforting spirituals being sung.

People have also reported that they've been touched by icy hands or felt someone—or something—momentarily brush past them, even though nobody else was around. Visitors have spoken of feeling like they were being watched, and some folks have been overcome by intense feelings of sadness or fear.

Hickory Hill gained a reputation as the house in which no one could stay overnight on the third floor. These stories began to circulate in the 1920s, when a famous ghost hunter named Hickman Whittington decided to rid the third floor of its ghosts. He reportedly hightailed it out of there after just a few hours and died soon after.

In 1966, two Marines attempted to spend the night on the third floor. But after hearing moaning and screaming and seeing strange shadow figures, they quickly fled the scene.

In 1978, as part of a Halloween ratings stunt, a television reporter named David Rogers managed to spend a night on the third floor of the Old Slave House, although he did say that his experience was extremely unsettling. He reported hearing many strange, unexplained sounds, and he later discovered voices on his tape recorder that he did not hear during his stay.

Before the Sisks finally gave up the house in 1996, Mrs. Sisk would not stay alone in the dwelling. Even on the warmest days, an unexplained chill could be felt in the house.

THE STORY CONTINUES...

Although Hickory Hill is listed on the National Register of Historic Places, it was closed to the public after the Sisks left, and its fate remains uncertain. The state of Illinois purchased it and is deciding whether or not to open it as a historical attraction. But whatever ultimately happens to the Old Slave House, it is almost certain that its tortured souls cannot—and will not—rest in peace. It seems that they'll continue to protest the terrible violence that was done to them until the end of time.

"Then away out in the woods I heard that kind of a sound that a ghost makes when it wants to tell about something that's on its mind and can't make itself understood, and so can't rest easy in its grave, and has to go about that way every night grieving."
—Mark Twain, *The Adventures of Huckleberry Finn*

WHEN THE GRAY MAN SPEAKS, YOU'D BETTER LISTEN

Pawleys Island is a small barrier island located along the coast of South Carolina. Only a handful of people live there year-round, and one of those permanent residents is the Gray Man. Many say that this restless spirit has no face, but that seems to be a minor issue. After all, when it comes to warning the living of impending doom, a pretty face—or any face at all—is hardly necessary.

APPARITION IDENTITY CRISIS

According to legend, before every major hurricane that has hit Pawleys Island since the early 1820s—including Hurricane Hugo in 1989—the Gray Man has appeared to certain folks there to warn them to leave before the approaching storm strikes. When they return after the storm, the people who encountered the Gray Man find their homes undamaged, while other buildings nearby have been destroyed.

The identity of the Gray Man is unknown, but there are several candidates. One theory suggests that it's the spirit of Percival Pawley, the island's first owner and its namesake. Others believe that the helpful specter is that of Plowden Charles Jennett Weston, a man whose former home is now the island's Pelican Inn.

But the more enchanting stories say that the Gray Man is the ghost of a young man who died for love. Stories about how he met his doom vary. One says that on his way to see his beloved, he fell into a bed of quicksand and died. Soon after, while the object of this man's affection was walking along the beach, a figure in gray approached her and told her to leave the island. She did, and that night a hurricane slammed into the area, destroying just about every home—except hers.

A different story concerns a woman who married another man after the man she truly loved died at sea. Later, she met a man who had survived a shipwreck off Pawleys Island, and she realized that he was her lost love—still very much alive. But he didn't take the news of her marriage very well. Brokenhearted, he slinked away and died soon after. And according to legend, ever since then, he's been warning folks to flee when they're in danger from a fast-approaching storm.

THE GHOSTLY LIFESAVER

No matter who this ghost was in life, he has supposedly appeared before hurricanes in 1822, 1893, 1916, 1954, 1955, and 1989. And for decades, local fishermen have told stories of the Gray Man appearing to them hours before the arrival of a sudden storm that would have put their lives in jeopardy.

The Gray Man is credited with saving many lives before the invention of modern forecasting equipment. In 1954, a couple was spending their honeymoon on the island when they heard a knock on their door at around 5 A.M. When the husband opened the door, he saw a figure in gray whose face was hidden by a gray hat. The man in gray said that the Red Cross had sent him to warn people to evacuate because a huge storm was heading for the island. Before the honeymooning husband could question him further, the man in gray vanished. Realizing that this was no ordinary Red Cross worker, the man and his new bride left the island immediately.

Later that evening, ferocious Hurricane Hazel struck the island with deadly force and winds gusting as high as 150 miles per hour. Hazel left thousands of homes destroyed and 95 people dead, but the newlywed couple was spared by the ghostly grace of the Gray Man.

A Ghost Who Keeps on Giving

The Gray Man apparently doesn't care much for modern technology—he was still on the job as recently as 1989. That year, just before Hurricane Hugo hit, a couple walking along the beach spotted the Gray Man. Although the phantom vanished before the couple could speak to him, his reputation preceded him, and the couple fled the island. When they returned, their home was the only one in the area that had not been devastated by the storm. This incident got the Gray Man a moment in the national spotlight when he was featured on an episode of *Unsolved Mysteries* the following year.

FRIGHTENING FACTS

- *Ernest Hemingway's former home in Key West, Florida, is now a tourist attraction—and the eternal home of his ghost. Visitors and staff members have heard him tapping away on his typewriter and witnessed him waving from a second-story window. He's also been seen nearby at Sloppy Joe's Bar. Apparently, ghosts even need to get out of the house and socialize once in a while.*

- *The James H. Quillen VA Medical Center in Mountain Home, Tennessee, opened in 1903 to care for veterans of the Civil War and the Spanish–American War. The most visible ghost there is a misty soldier in a Spanish–American War uniform who floats and glides around outside.*

- *In 1840, Gertrude Tredwell was born in the building that's now the Merchant's House Museum on East 4th Street in New York City. She lived there her entire life and died there at age 93. When a person is so attached to a place, it's understandable that he or she would be reluctant to leave it. That seems to be the case with Gertrude, whose spirit still keeps a watchful eye over her eternal home, as numerous people have witnessed.*

- *From the late 1880s through the mid-1930s, Jerome, Arizona, was a mining boomtown. In the late 1800s, while two miners were fighting over a woman, they accidentally stabbed her to death. These days, her ghost (among others) haunts the nearly deserted town.*

Voodoo Meets Boo! in "The Big Easy"

New Orleans is often called America's most haunted city. It is well known for its famous Mardi Gras celebration and endless party on Bourbon Street. But the city's origins give it a supernatural reputation. In 1718, the French founded the city where swampland meets Native American burial grounds. Toss in a few major fires, a bunch of murders, and an epidemic or two, and there are sure to be some ghosts roaming the city. So whether you plan to visit or just like a good ghost story, here's a look at some of the most haunted places that "The Big Easy" has to offer.

The Andrew Jackson Hotel

Don't stay at the Andrew Jackson Hotel unless you're willing to share your room with a few uninvited guests. The hotel was built on the site of a boarding school that burned down in the 1700s, and guests have heard the shouting and laughter of the five boys who died in the blaze. A courthouse was later built on the site, and war hero Andrew Jackson was tried there for obstruction of justice. Perhaps he hung around—some visitors have reported seeing the specter of "Old Hickory" himself.

The Beauregard-Keyes House

A prime stop on New Orleans ghost tours, the historic Beauregard–Keyes House boasts a rather sophisticated spirit. As ghosts go, a world-class chess master sounds pretty tame— but an *insane* chess master is an entirely different story. In the late 1870s, Paul Morphy (the chess champ) was living at the Beauregard–Keyes House when he apparently suffered a breakdown and ran down the street stark naked and swinging an ax. In his quieter moments, Paul enjoyed playing the piano, so an odd combination of screaming and piano music is now heard at the historic house on some nights.

In addition, a mob massacre took place on the property in 1908. Since then, visitors have smelled gunpowder and heard gunshots in the garden.

BOURBON STREET

A lot of fun can be had on Bourbon Street—even for the dead. Spirits have been seen pounding each other with curtain rods up and down the street. Because of its unique jumble of cultures, religions, and politics, New Orleans has had a diverse history. Therefore, it's not clear who the apparitions were in life, or even from what time period they hail. But dodge those curtain rods, just to be safe.

FLANAGAN'S PUB

In the 1920s and '30s, the building that is now home to Flanagan's Pub was Ruffino's Bakery. Its owners were involved in the Sicilian mob, and it is rumored that members of the Irish labor union were tortured (and sometimes killed) there for information that would allow the Sicilians to take over their organization. Many pub employees and patrons have witnessed a spectral man walk out of the kitchen and through the bar. Several employees have also seen pots and pans fly off their hooks and utensils move on their own. And during a paranormal investigation, a spirit seemed eager to speak to a former employee. Whoever this phantom was in life, it seemed to trust the former employee and desperately wanted her to return.

LE RICHELIEU HOTEL

In 1802, after the French reclaimed Louisiana from Spain, Spanish soldiers were executed for treason at the site where Le Richelieu Hotel now stands. The men who lost their lives there are said to walk the grounds late at night. Look for spectral men in Spanish uniforms lingering near the bar or swimming pool.

CITY PARK GOLF COURSE

Good golfing manners require people to be quiet when golfers hit the ball, and ghosts can certainly be silent when they need to be. But at City Park Golf Course, golfers may break the silence with screams when they approach the 18th green of the East Course. That's where a ghost hangs out. Even worse is the haunting that many have experienced on the South Course, where golfers claim to hear muffled female voices and laughing nearby, followed by the sharp crack of a gunshot and a woman shouting, "I'm hit." This seems to be a residual haunting or ghostly reenactment of a death that took place near the course in the early 1960s. No one was ever charged with the shooting.

French Quarter

Numerous spirits are certainly present in New Orleans's historic French Quarter, but one of the most famous specters there is the Chicken Man. A voodoo practitioner commonly seen in the 1970s and '80s, the Chicken Man was said to have approached people on the street offering goodies from his bag—which was tied with a dangling chicken claw. He hadn't been seen in the area for quite some time, but after Hurricane Katrina in 2005, visitors began seeing him in the French Quarter—in spirit form. One woman said that a man on the street offered her a bag tied with his signature gnarled chicken claw. The Chicken Man is back!

Lafitte Guest House

You might want to check out Room 21 at the Lafitte Guest House, but you may have trouble sleeping there. Before it became a bed-and-breakfast, the Lafitte Guest House was a single-family home, and two girls died in that room. One girl died of yellow fever during the great epidemic of 1853, and many years later, her sister hung herself in the same room. Grief-stricken, their mother lived out the rest of her days in that bedroom, where she died of natural causes. Employees and guests have reported a feeling of complete despair in Room 21, along with the sound of the mother crying.

Le Petit Theatre du Vieux Carre

Before you enter Le Petit Theatre du Vieux Carre, check out the upper part of the building where it overlooks the courtyard. It is there that many people have seen the ghost of Caroline, a young woman who, in 1924, jumped to her death wearing a wedding dress—her costume for a play. Cold spots chill guests, and many have seen Caroline's reflection in the fountain at night.

Caroline may have some company. A spectral old man dressed in formal attire from the 1800s has been spotted in the second-story seating area. But when staff members search for him, he mysteriously disappears. Actors and stagehands have also felt cold hands on their shoulders, had props go missing, and watched a smoke machine turn on by itself.

THE MORGUE BAR

With a name like the Morgue Bar, you'd expect some paranormal activity to occur at this establishment—and it does. As a former funeral home, the Morgue Bar has seen many lifeless bodies pass through its doors—especially in 1853, when more than 10,000 people died in the city due to a yellow fever epidemic. Many modern patrons have seen apparitions from that era belly up to the bar. Another ghost that seems ever-present is a former mortician's daughter, who, in life, was known for stealing jewelry from the dead bodies that her father worked on. Unfortunately, death hasn't reformed her. She frequently "borrows" items from the bar's female patrons when they visit the restroom, which formerly served as a storage room for bodies. As long as you keep your belongings close at hand, you should be safe from her antics.

THE SUPERDOME

Many modern ghosts haunt New Orleans, and the Superdome is a popular hangout for old and new spirits alike. After Hurricane Katrina pummeled the city in August 2005, thousands of people were sent to the Superdome for safety. But it turned out to be a nightmare for many. Several murders and two suicides occurred there, as well as many deaths from natural causes. Is it any wonder that ghosts roam this stadium?

In addition, the Superdome was allegedly built on the site of an old cemetery, and workers supposedly dug up bones and caskets when the stadium was under construction. Today, apparitions have been spotted during football games played there, especially at night. It seems all the morbid activity that has occurred under this domed roof has left an imprint on the famous building.

TAKE A WALK ON THE OTHER SIDE

At England's Falstaff's Experience, ghosts—and the possession of visitors—are routine occurrences.

By day, the Falstaff's Experience in Stratford-upon-Avon, England, is an amusing historical and ghost-themed attraction. Costumed mannequins, coffins dripping fake blood, and a re-creation of a "plague cottage" are among the displays that provide chills and thrills to visitors. At night, however, the atmosphere can turn sinister. Dozens of spirits freely roam both floors of the building and appear on the staircases between them. Only ghost hunters with nerves of steel should join one of the "midnight vigils" at the Falstaff's Experience.

A Beastly Barn

The land under the Falstaff's Experience is believed to have been a cemetery in the sixth century. As Christianity became popular in Britain, early burial grounds such as this were typically dismissed as pagan and built over. By the 12th century, the site included a house and a barn used for trading sheep and wool. However, in the 14th century, the sheep and their wool carried fleas infested with bubonic plague to the area. Thousands of people died. Their homes became known as plague cottages.

Later, the barn and house belonged to William Shrieve, one of King Henry VIII's archers. Even today, many people refer to the site as "Shrieve's House," particularly because his ghost has been seen there.

During the English Civil War in the mid-1600s, the barn was used as a hospital, and some people think the spirits of many wounded soldiers have never left the building. The soldiers died slow, bloody, feverish deaths in an era when painkillers barely existed. When the TV show *Most Haunted Live* filmed at the Falstaff's Experience in 2004, medium Derek Acorah was possessed by a soldier whose arm was being amputated. From Acorah's slurred speech and drunken singing, it seems that the soldier's only painkiller was liquor. Today, the barn is known as one of the most haunted places in Britain.

Midnight Vigils

During the midnight vigils at the Falstaff's Experience, visitors explore several rooms of the old barn before they're led up the stairs. People often report feeling a sense of dread as they climb these steps. Some even leave the tour before reaching the upper floor. Many guests describe invisible hands grabbing them around the ankles. Some have seen bloody soldiers. Others sense a feeling of imminent danger or even death. For those who make it up the stairs, even more frightening experiences await.

Visitors have seen streetlights shining through an open window several feet above the haunted staircase. This seems normal enough—until the tour guide turns on the building's interior lights to reveal that there is no window. Some believe the image is from an earlier time when a window *was* there. Others feel it may be a portal to a ghostly dimension.

Sharpened Senses

In the Middle Ages, John Davies traveled the countryside sharpening knives and axes. The weapons came in handy because Davies was one of England's first serial killers. When Davies's ghost appears at the Falstaff's Experience, he's described as an average-looking man wearing a white shirt and brown trousers. Of particular note are the bloody knife he appears to be carrying and the stench of his breath. Women are especially vulnerable near the staircase, where they may encounter Davies's malicious spirit. His ghost has been known to frighten women by breathing on them— usually on the cheek or neck—near the staircase or on the upper floor of the barn.

Playful Lucy

As visitors move past the staircase and onto the upper level, they'll come to Lucy's room. Little Lucy is a mischievous ghost-child whose mother was accused of witchcraft and killed in the 1700s. The young girl was questioned, tortured, and killed, but she never betrayed her mother.

Today, Lucy allegedly pats visitors' hair, tugs at jewelry, and moves small items around her room. People have taken off their necklaces and held them out, only to find ghostly hands pulling at the jewelry. It's as if Lucy never gets tired of playing. But her innocence is in sharp contrast to some other spirits at the Falstaff's Experience.

Ghostly Slideshow

Visitors courageous enough to stand directly beneath the upstairs smoke alarm may see something startling. In the eerie green light from the alarm, a visitor's appearance is often trans-formed to resemble a ghost. A few seconds later, another ghost manifests, and so on. People have seen as many as six different apparitions of varying ages, genders, and hairstyles. Some wear jewelry, and even their clothing may be visible.

Those who volunteer to participate in the experiment are not permanently possessed. Apparently, the ghosts are simply using the person as a backdrop to project their images. Most volunteers describe a sense of imbalance, saying that the experience isn't scary, just very strange.

DON'T LOOK BACK

After leaving a room at the Falstaff's Experience, it's best not to go back into it. Visitors who have returned to a room have described feeling disoriented. Some ghost hunters encountered a hooded figure when they returned to Lucy's room. Others felt as if the furniture was floating around them or they were sinking into another dimension. Videos taken by visitors have shown unexplained figures moving in front of the camera. It's as if the ghosts are willing to let people pass through their home, but they want them to keep moving. The one exception is John Davies, who often follows guests from room to room until they leave the building.

It's pretty safe to say that the Falstaff's Experience is one of the few places in the world where you can get a sense of what it's like on "the Other Side."

THIS CHICAGO THEATER
IS NEVER COMPLETELY EMPTY

*When Chicago's Iroquois Theatre opened for business,
at least one person described the place as "a death
trap." But according to records, the building was
in full compliance with the city's fire code, and
advertisements billed it as "absolutely fireproof."
Unfortunately, that first description proved to be true.*

FALSE ADVERTISING

When the Iroquois Theatre opened in November 1903, it
was easy to feel safe while sitting underneath its ornate,
60-foot-high ceiling and among its white marble walls and
grand staircases. However, patrons didn't know that when
the theater was constructed, its owners had cut corners to
open in time for the holiday season.

In their eagerness to open, the owners of the Iroquois failed
to install sprinkler systems, and not all of the fire escapes
were completed when the theater opened. In addition, exit
signs were either missing or obscured by thick drapes, there
were no backstage phones or fire buckets, and no fire alarm
system was in place. In fact, the only fire-fighting equipment
in the theater was a few canisters of a chemical product
called Kilfyre. The owners had even skimped on the stage's
safety curtain. Instead of using fireproof asbestos to make
it, the owners saved about $50 by having the builders use a

blend of asbestos, cotton, and wood pulp—cotton and wood pulp are not exactly fireproof. But at the time, it was not uncommon for building inspectors and city officials to accept bribes to look the other way as construction crews ignored one safety law after another.

"A DEATH TRAP"

On December 30, barely a month after the theater opened, vaudeville star Eddie Foy and his company were onstage performing the musical *Mr. Blue Beard* to a standing-room-only crowd that was estimated to be around 2,000 people—a few hundred more than the theater could safely hold.

At the beginning of the second act, a light sent a spark onto a drape hanging on a wall near the stage. The orchestra stopped playing, but Foy urged the audience to remain calm and stay in their seats. Even after the flames jumped to pieces of scenery that were hanging in the rafters—most of which were painted with highly flammable oil-based paint—Foy stayed onstage and begged the audience to remain calm and exit the theater in an orderly fashion. But Foy was no fool. He knew that when the scenery in the rafters caught fire, the situation was going to get a lot worse.

Above and behind him, the fire spread quickly, and the cast and crew dashed for a backstage exit. Lighting gear jammed the fire curtain after it dropped only a few feet, which left the audience fully exposed to the flames on the stage.

When performers tried to open the back door, they discovered that the ventilation system had been nailed shut. This kept the cold winter air from getting inside, but it also effectively turned the building into a gigantic chimney. The minute the door was opened, a back draft turned the flames on the stage into what eyewitnesses described as a "balloon of fire." This massive fireball shot through the auditorium, burning some people to death right where they stood.

Naturally, the crowd panicked and ran for the fire exits, which the owners had locked to keep people from sneaking into the theater without paying. Those who weren't trampled trying to reach the fire exits ran for the front doors, hoping to rush out onto the street. But the doors opened in toward the lobby, not out toward the street, so rather than escaping through the doors, the people crashed into them, and then into each other. More people died from being crushed in the chaos than from burns or inhaling smoke.

Meanwhile, the only hallway that led downstairs from the balcony was blocked by a metal gate that was placed there to keep people from sneaking into better seats. This trapped those unfortunate people in the upper reaches of the burning building. Some tried to jump from the balcony to escape. Others opened the balcony's fire exit, which was miraculously kept unlocked. However, by the time those who opened the door realized that there *was* no fire escape behind the door, the crowd was pushing too hard for them to turn back. They were shoved out the door and dropped nearly 60 feet into the alley below. By the time the situation had calmed down, more than a hundred people had fallen to their demise in what newspapers called "Death Alley."

In the Wake of Tragedy

The exact number of lives lost in the Iroquois Theatre fire is uncertain. Around 600 people are known to have perished there, which is twice the number that died in the Great Chicago Fire of 1871. But the actual number is probably much higher because many families picked up their dead relatives before they could be counted. To this day, the fire at the Iroquois Theatre is the deadliest single-building fire in U.S. history. The silver lining was that the use of steel fire curtains, clearly marked exits, and doors that swing out toward the street all became mandatory as a result of the tragedy at the Iroquois Theatre.

Following the incident, a number of city officials were brought to trial for gross negligence, but they all got off on technicalities. The only people who were ever successfully prosecuted for crimes surrounding the Iroquois fire were a few of the crooks who broke into the theater to shimmy rings off fingers, yank necklaces from necks, and dig money out of the pockets of the dead. (And the vast majority of those people were never prosecuted, either.)

THE BUILDING MAY BE GONE, BUT THE GHOSTS REMAIN

Ghost sightings at the Iroquois Theatre began before the flames had even stopped smoldering. Photos taken of the auditorium shortly after the fire contain strange blobs of light and mist that some believe are the spirits of the dead.

The theater was soon repaired and reopened, and it operated for another 20 years before it was torn down. In its place, a new venue—the Oriental Theatre—was erected in 1926. For decades, it was one of Chicago's premier movie theaters, but it fell on hard times in the 1970s. The Oriental Theatre finally shut its doors in 1981, and it seemed as though the Iroquois and its tragic tale had faded into Chicago's history.

But since 1998, when the Oriental Theatre reopened to host touring Broadway shows, employees have found that the ghosts have stuck around. During rehearsals, spectators are frequently seen in the balcony. But when staff members go up to ask them to leave, they find the balcony empty.

Many people who work in the building have reported seeing the specter of a woman in a tutu. This is thought to be the ghost of Nellie Reed, an aerialist who was in position high above the audience when the fire broke out. Although she was rescued from her perch, she suffered severe burns and died a few days later.

Other actors and crew members have encountered the ghost of a young girl who makes her presence known by giggling and flushing one of the toilets backstage. Her happy laugh has been picked up on audio recorders on more than one occasion and can often be heard in the hallways next to the main auditorium.

Staff members who work late at night, after all the theater-goers have left the building, have reported seeing shadowy blobs that they call "soft shapes." These mysterious forms are seen zipping through the empty auditorium toward the places where the fire exits would have been in 1903.

The ghosts in the theater may not only be spirits from the fire. Female staff members have reportedly been harassed and threatened by an otherworldly male voice in one of the sub-basements located far below the street. Historians suggest that this ghost may be from the 1800s, when the section of Randolph Street where the theater now stands was known as "Hairtrigger Block" and was home to the rowdiest gambling parlors in town.

Sometimes, after a building is torn down, its ghosts seem to go away. But other times, as seems to be the case with the Iroquois Theatre, they only get louder and more active.

"Lotz" of Ghosts Gather at the Carter House

Franklin, Tennessee, which is located about 20 miles south of Nashville, has a population of 64,000—unless you count its ghosts. The site of what some historians consider the bloodiest one-day battle of the Civil War, Franklin is rich with history—and restless spirits. It seems that many of the soldiers who lost their lives in that famous battle are still hanging around the city.

Before the Blood

In 1830, Fountain Branch Carter built a beautiful home in the heart of Franklin. In 1858, Johann Lotz constructed his own house across the street on land that he'd purchased from Carter. Both were blissfully unaware of what would occur there just a few years later.

After the fall of Nashville in 1862, Franklin became a Union military post. In 1864, in an attempt to "take the bull by the horns," the Confederate army decided to attack the enemy head-on in Franklin, hoping to drive General Sherman's army north. It didn't quite work out that way, though. Instead, during the Battle of Franklin on November 30, 1864, more than 4,000 lives were lost. Because the battlefield was small, the concentration of bloodshed was very high. And most of it took place right in front of the Lotz and Carter homes.

THE BATTLE BEGINS

When the Confederate troops arrived in town, Union General Jacob Cox took over the Carter House as his base of operations. Fearing for their lives, the Carter and Lotz families sought safety in the basement during the five long hours of the battle. In all, 23 people crowded into the cellar. They all survived, and when the fighting was over, both houses were converted into field hospitals. Surgeries, amputations, and death filled the days and weeks that followed. Between the violence and the pain that occurred there, it's no wonder that some of the dead never found peace.

One of the men who was killed during the battle was Tod Carter, Fountain's son and a Confederate soldier who was thrilled to be heading home. He was wounded just 300 feet from the front door of his boyhood home and was taken to his sister's bedroom, where he later died. Some say that his spirit remains there today.

HISTORY COMES TO LIFE

In 1953, the Carter House was opened to the public as a museum. Its eight acres stand as a tribute to the battle that took place there so long ago. If you look closely, more than a thousand bullet holes can be found on the property. The Lotz House—which opened to the public in 2008—bears its share of scars as well. Bloodstains are evident throughout, and a round indentation in the wood floor is a reminder of a cannonball that crashed through the roof and fell through a second-story bedroom before landing in the parlor on the first floor, leaving a charred path in its wake.

In the Spirit of Things

Visitors to the Carter House have reported seeing the specter of Tod Carter sitting on a bed and standing in the hallway. His sister Annie has also been spotted there. She's blamed for playful pranks such as rolling a ball along the floor and causing objects to appear and disappear. But then again, the mischief-maker might be the spirit of one of the other children who took refuge in the cellar during the battle. Staff members and visitors have reported feeling the sensation of a child tugging at their sleeves, and one worker even saw a phantom child walking down the staircase.

The ghosts of soldiers and other family members may be responsible for some of the other unusual phenomena experienced in the house, such as furniture moving on its own, doors slamming, and apparitions peering through the windows.

Not to be outdone, the ghosts at the Lotz House manifest as phantom voices and household items that move on their own or come up missing. Although they haven't been identified, they seem to be civilian spirits rather than military ones.

It's tough sharing a space with so many ghosts, but the staff members are used to it, and they're happy to share the history—and the spirits—with visitors who stop by on the Franklin on Foot Ghost Tour. But don't worry: These lively spirits have never followed anyone home—at least not yet!

BOBBY MACKEY'S: GHOSTS, SPIRITS, AND COUNTRY MUSIC

Just over the Ohio River from downtown Cincinnati is the town of Wilder, Kentucky, home of Bobby Mackey's—a country-music nightclub and allegedly one of the most haunted locations in the United States. Over the years, the property is said to have seen such atrocities as a beheading, a poisoning, a suicide, numerous unsolved murders, and even a case of possession. On top of all that, some say there's an entrance to hell in the basement.

HELL'S GATE

The first building that is believed to have stood on the property now occupied by Bobby Mackey's was a slaughterhouse, which operated from the 1850s until the late 1880s. During that time, it was said to have been so busy that the ground floor was often literally soaked with blood. To alleviate that, a well was dug in the basement. This allowed the blood to be washed off the floor and carried out to the nearby river. Needless to say, gallons upon gallons of blood and other assorted matter were dumped into the well. Perhaps that's why legend has it that after the slaughterhouse closed, a satanic cult used the well as part of its rituals. Some even claim that these rituals opened a portal to the Other Side, an entrance that—to this day—has yet to be closed.

An Unspeakable Crime

On February 1, 1896, the headless body of young Pearl Bryan was found less than two miles from the site of the former slaughterhouse. It was later discovered that Pearl's boyfriend, Scott Jackson, and his friend, Alonzo Walling, had murdered her. The two men were arrested, but they refused to reveal the location of Pearl's head. In March 1897, both men were hanged for the crime without ever disclosing the location of Pearl's head. Most people believed that they threw the head into the old slaughterhouse well. Perhaps that's why Pearl Bryan's ghost is seen wandering around inside Bobby Mackey's, both with and without her head. And although Scott Jackson and Alonzo Walling did not take their last breaths on the property, it is believed that their spirits are stuck there too. They have both been seen throughout the building, but Scott's ghost seems to be more active—and angry. Those who have encountered his ghost—usually near the well in the basement—say that it's a dark and unhappy spirit.

Gangsters and Unsolved Murders

Shortly after the executions of Jackson and Walling, the former slaughterhouse was torn down, leaving only the well.

In the 1920s, the building now known as Bobby Mackey's was built on the property directly over the well. During Prohibition—when the sale of alcohol was illegal—it served as a speakeasy and gambling den where several people were killed. Eventually, the building was shut down and cleared out—presumably of everything except the restless spirits.

In 1933, after Prohibition ended, E. A. "Buck" Brady bought the building and turned it into a nightclub called The Primrose. Soon after, powerful gangsters began showing up at the club trying to scare Buck into giving them a cut of his profits. But Buck refused to be intimidated. All this came to a head on August 5, 1946, when Buck and gangster Albert "Red" Masterson were involved in a shootout. After that, Buck decided that he was done. After many years of being bullied by gangsters, Buck sold The Primrose. But as he handed over the keys, he allegedly cursed the building, saying that because he couldn't run a successful business there, no one should.

Today, the apparitions of both Buck Brady and Red Masterson are seen inside Bobby Mackey's. Buck's ghost has been identified from photographs of him. And even though he cursed the building, his spirit seems harmless enough. Red's ghost, on the other hand, has been described as "not friendly" and has been blamed for some of the alleged attacks on bar patrons.

Johanna

After Buck sold The Primrose, it reopened as a nightclub called The Latin Quarter. According to legend, Johanna, the daughter of the new owner, fell in love with (and became pregnant by) Robert Randall, one of the club's singers. After Johanna's father found out about her pregnancy, he had Randall killed. When Johanna learned what her father had done, she unsuccessfully tried to poison him and then killed herself in the basement of the building.

Johanna's ghost is seen throughout the building, but it is most often sighted on the top floor and in the stairwells, where she will either push or hug people. She is also said to hang out in the Spotlight Room, a secret place in the attic where she allegedly wrote a poem on the wall before killing herself. Even when you can't see Johanna's apparition, you can tell that she's around by the inexplicable scent of roses.

One of the strangest phenomena attributed to Johanna's ghost is that the turned-off (and unplugged) jukebox sometimes springs to life, playing "The Anniversary Waltz"—despite the fact that the record is not even in the machine.

Bobby Mackey's Music World

In the spring of 1978, musician Bobby Mackey purchased the building. Besides operating as a bar, Bobby Mackey's has a stage and a dance floor and has featured performances by many popular country music acts over the years.

Shortly after her husband purchased the building, Janet Mackey was working in the upstairs apartment when she was shoved out of the room toward the stairs while being told to "Get out" by a spirit that she later identified as Alonzo Walling. After that, Janet refused to set foot in the room. So Bobby hired Carl Lawson as a caretaker and allowed him to stay in the apartment.

After moving in, Carl heard strange noises and saw shadow figures moving around the bar late at night. Believing that the spirits were coming in through the well in the basement, he threw holy water down the hole. Carl claimed that he became possessed as a result and was only able to break free from the demon's grasp after an exorcism was performed.

In 1993, a man sued Bobby Mackey's bar claiming that while he was in the men's room, he was punched and kicked by a "dark-haired apparition" wearing a cowboy hat. The victim stated that he might have angered the spirit because he dared it to appear shortly before being attacked. Although the lawsuit was thrown out, it did result in the now-famous sign that hangs above the front doors of Bobby Mackey's, which alerts guests to the possibility that the building may be haunted and that they are entering at their own risk.

PRIME-TIME GHOSTS

Bobby Mackey repeatedly turned down requests to have his bar investigated by ghost hunters. But in 2008, he allowed the popular TV show *Ghost Adventures* to film an episode there, and it resulted in some interesting footage. Among other things, investigators encountered odd cold spots and claimed to have heard the voice of a woman. While using the men's room, investigator Nick Groff heard banging noises, which startled him so much that he ran out of the restroom without zipping up his pants. The team also captured some odd video of what appeared to be a man in a cowboy hat moving around in the basement.

But the episode will forever be remembered as the one in which ghost hunter Zak Bagans claimed to have been attacked by a demonic entity after challenging the evil forces in the basement. As proof, Zak proudly displayed three scratch marks on his back. He called it one of the scariest things he had ever experienced. But that didn't stop *Ghost Adventures* from returning to Bobby Mackey's in 2010. The evil entities there were also back with a vengeance.

Other investigators spending time at Bobby Mackey's might be a bit disappointed if they don't experience as much para-normal activity as the *Ghost Adventures* team did, but that doesn't mean that the spirits aren't around. For example, when a group from Ghosts of Ohio visited Bobby Mackey's, the investigation seemed uneventful. But when the team members reviewed their audio afterward, they found that a recorder set up near the infamous well picked up a voice clearly saying, "It hurts."